Young Pathfinder 8

A CILT series for primary language teachers

Grammar is fun

Lydia Biriotti

Drawings by Lydia Biriotti

D0996260

CiLT The National
Centre for
Languages

The views expressed in this book are those of the author and do not necessarily represent the views of CILT.

Acknowledgements

This book is the culmination of many years of work teaching French to young children. Along the way, many people have given me invaluable encouragement, among them Grace Armbruster as long ago as the late 1970s, and more recently Ian McGregor, John Hubbard and Patricia McLagan.

The text itself is the product of many versions and revisions, and I would like to acknowledge the tireless efforts of Catherine Dey in helping me to prepare the first draft. The help of my husband Ralph Biriotti and my sons, Maurice and Victor, has also been decisive.

Over the years, I have benefited from a great deal of support, notably from all of my family and from my outstanding colleagues at the Junior Branch of University College School. Finally, the book would never have emerged if it had not been for that source of endless creative energy: the children I have taught.

First published 1999
by the Centre for Information on Language Teaching and Research (CILT)
20 Bedfordbury, London, WC2N 4LB.

Copyright © Centre for Information on Language Teaching and Research 1999
ISBN 1 902031 24 5

Cover by Neil Alexander
Cover illustrations by Genna Hollins
Interior illustrations by Lydia Biriotti
Printed in the United Kingdom by Hobbs the Printers Ltd, Totton, Hampshire SO40 3WX

CILT Publications are available from: **Central Books**, 99 Wallis Rd, London E9 5LN. Tel: 0845 458 9910. Fax: 0845 458 9912. Book trade representation (UK and Ireland): **Broadcast Book Services**, Charter House, 27a London Rd, Croydon CR0 2RE. Tel: 020 8681 8949. Fax: 020 8688 0615.

Contents

Introduction: Getting the basics right

Over the past twenty years, there has been a proliferation of texts that provide approaches to the teaching of French for children. Although there is a rich variety of different products on the market, most recent approaches are intended to develop fluency by focusing on language learning as 'fun' as opposed to being rigorously grammatical.

The traditional grammatical approach to teaching English and foreign languages has been in decline. The failings in general of this methodology were thought to be that:

- it is too dry, academic or impenetrable for children brought up on a diet of video games, television and 'youth culture';

- it is based on approaches that seem more akin to the teaching of so-called 'dead languages' than modern European languages;

- it does not inspire children to gain the skills they need to feel confident in a living language.

The trend is towards creating texts and methodologies that focus on developing confidence, generating 'fun' and enjoyment, and fostering fluency and a lack of inhibition. This approach has certain failings too. In particular:

- it means that children have little basic understanding of the language on which to base new vocabulary, forms or phrases;

- it fails to supply the basic structures of language acquisition for children upon which they can base the study of other languages later in life (one of Latin's much vaunted advantages in a previous era);

- it can lead to a lack of accuracy and a poor foundation in the use of language.

The period of a child's development from seven to eleven years of age is a crucial time for the acquisition of skills and knowledge. The recent drive to offer language teaching to this age group has been met with a lack of suitable care and attention over the content of the provision. Grammar is an essential component of success in language learning for these young children. So is 'fun', without which motivation is impossible to generate, and the relevance of what pupils are learning escapes them.

The challenge is to find a way of facilitating the acquisition of a secure grammatical understanding that is not only painless but also enjoyable. Enjoyment is not antithetical to order. On the contrary, pupils who learn a language in a structured fashion from the outset are less likely to feel lost in the language and more likely to express themselves with confidence and flair. This implies a disciplined approach right from the first lesson.

It is important to teach children vocabulary with some understanding of the basic linguistic structures in which that vocabulary will acquire meaning. New words, new structures and new concepts must be grouped together in ways that make sense of the language. That is the teacher's responsibility.

Right from the start children should be made aware of similarities and differences between their language and the target language. Children learning a second language do not start with a clean linguistic slate. Teaching a child a new language is not the same as allowing a new-born child to acquire its native tongue.

- Accuracy should be encouraged at every stage. Language learning is achieved step by step: each step can be wonderfully entertaining, and getting the basics right at an early stage will facilitate accuracy and fluency later on.

- Acquiring accuracy can be compatible with a 'natural' approach: fluency and accuracy can go hand in hand.

- Anything can be taught in an engaging and entertaining way with enough imagination.

Any new idea can seem alienating when it is first introduced, and this is best overcome by carefully explaining and illustrating how and why grammar rules in another language are different, in a way which makes them easily understood and remembered. Once grasped, they form the basis of successful language learning.

The principle underlying this approach is simple. When children learn a second language, they are already conditioned—albeit subconsciously — by the rules governing their mother tongue. In order for a class to become comfortable with new ideas and to understand them fully, children should constantly be given the chance to practise what they have learnt. It is tempting to assume that if they give the correct answer initially, they have understood the grammatical rule: this is not always the case. Often what is needed is a practical approach, which takes the class through the new rules and their implications, stage by stage.

Fluency and accuracy can be encouraged if they are developed in a way that captures the imagination of the class. Several examples, games and exercises can be presented as variations on a theme, with the simplest of exercises and competitions serving to illustrate some of the more complex grammatical rules both clearly and easily.

CILT

1.   Understanding the notion of gender

One of the most important aspects of foreign language learning is understanding the notion of gender. For English speaking children, the idea that everyday words can be either masculine or feminine is likely to be a completely alien concept. It is not something they can be expected simply to pick up on, without some concerted effort on the part of a teacher to get the point across.

How best to introduce this idea of gender can be a contentious issue. There is a tension between traditional approaches which offer examples rather than explanation, and newer techniques which are more ready to dispense with issues of gender altogether, preferring to focus on making classes fun, rather than on grammatical accuracy. An ideal approach would be a method combining both aspects, broaching the subject of gender without losing that element of fun which captures the imagination.

The traditional method of making gender distinction is to put an article (*un/une, le/la*) before each noun in a list of vocabulary. However, attaching genders to words can seem an arbitrary process for children who come across this idea for the first time. Simply adding the relevant gender to a list of nouns fails to establish a pattern which can become recognisable — after all, from an English speaking child's point of view, why should gender be applied to words on the basis of an arbitrary set of rules?

While old-fashioned approaches stress individual word genders in rather a dry way, relying on children learning the examples 'parrot-fashion', the contemporary methods may sacrifice accuracy for the sake of fluency and are no better.

Familiarising children with the notion of the importance of gender will be invaluable as the course progresses. A class which is aware of the concept of gender will, for example, have far less trouble understanding later on in the course that adjectives agree with the gender of the noun they qualify.

Stressing the importance of using genders correctly from the outset is not only a useful first step for teaching French. Once English speaking children are aware of the concept of gender in the target language, they can go on to apply the same principles to other European languages they may come across in the future. And since most children begin their introduction to foreign languages through their French lessons, it is never too early to talk about gender, especially if the message is conveyed in a clear and entertaining way.

With all this in mind, the trick is to devise a method for introducing the concept of gender which would combine an emphasis on accuracy with fun, stressing the gender groups of nouns in an entertaining way. There is no way of side-stepping the role of memory here: but that does not mean that the process needs to be dry.

MEMORY GAMES

The method described in this book uses memory games played with the whole class, illustrating how gender works simply and effectively. These games are played in English at the very outset of the course before any French vocabulary is taught.

The games take the form of a series of short stories in English told by the teacher, while the class listens. Each story involves a collection of nouns which the class has to remember in the right order.

Before each story, the teacher gives a pointer about the gender of the nouns to remember — the gender of the nouns depends on whether the story is about a little boy or a little girl. If the story is about a little girl, all the nouns they are to look out for will be feminine; if it is about a little boy, the nouns will be masculine. The following example may be adapted to introduce any new group of related words:

THE LITTLE GIRL'S STORY

The teacher tells the story **in English,** listing all the nouns **in French** in a column on the board. and pronounces each French word as it is written up.

> The list
> on the board
> would
> therefore be:

A little girl opened the door and walked into the classroom.
She looked at her watch. It was one o'clock.
She went over to the window to look outside.
It was raining.
She sat on a chair.
She opened her pencil-case.
There were two things inside. A rubber and a ruler.
She put them down on the table.
On the table she found a calculator, a box,
a television, a radio, a watch and a CD player.

une porte	une trousse	une boîte
une classe	une gomme	une télévision
une montre	une règle	une radio
une fenêtre	une table	une platine-laser
une chaise	une calculatrice	

The children are encouraged to pay close attention to the story as it is told and are then asked to repeat the list of English words in the order they appeared in the story, in English. Each of the children in turn is invited to come to the front of the class and recite the list of objects in English with his back to the board. Each time the pupil successfully names one of the objects in English, the teacher says it in French, exaggerating the sound of the article — *UNE*. The first to remember all the objects in the story in the correct order wins the game. In this way **children learn the gender of a group of words in English while repeatedly listening to the French word pronounced correctly**.

CiLT

The game can then be repeated with a story about a boy that introduces nouns that are masculine in gender. When the games have been played, a game of '*Pigeon vole*' is an excellent way of checking that they have understood the exercise. The entire class gives an English word either 'thumbs up' or 'thumbs down' according to whether they think the word was in the story of the girl or the story of the boy.

Only when the teacher is satisfied that pupils have learned to group these specific words together are they asked to memorise the words in French, which they have probably already assimilated by a sort of passive learning in this phase of the exercise.

It is crucial to stress the importance of pronunciation — especially the pronunciation of the all-important French article. It is essential to make sure that they make a great distinction between the pronunciation of '*un*' and '*une*'. To pronounce '*une*' you have to purse your lips. To pronounce '*un*' you just open your mouth in a slightly disgusted fashion! Start therefore by practising these two sounds. The sound '*ane*', which is often used as an indeterminate in-between syllable for the unsure is not acceptable! The same attention to detail in pronunciation must later be applied to '*le*' and '*la*'.

Memory tests, which require this degree of concentration, are a familiar feature of children's games and provide an effective introduction to the idea of gender. The class does not need to distinguish between words of different genders at first as this is already done for them — all the words introduced are linked together and by remembering that they belong to one story or another, the children automatically know which gender they are. In this way they become familiar with the notion that words in French have different genders, but are not put off by the apparently random nature of gender allocation which a list of words on its own suggests.

Here are some more examples of linked vocabulary exercises:

En ville

A boy who worked in a restaurant met up with his friend in the park. They couldn't decide what to do.
The friend wanted to go to the theatre, he wanted to go to the cinema.
They started shouting and fighting.
He was badly hurt.
Eventually his friend was arrested and taken to the hospital.
He was taken to the police station.

In this case, the following list would appear on the board:

le restaurant
le jardin public
le théâtre
le cinéma
le commissariat
l'hôpital

Depending on the group of children involved, it may be appropriate to continue to use this technique for new vocabulary learning beyond the introductory class. For a more advanced group, learning new vocabulary in the same way, a story might look like this:

The French list on the board would look like this:

Two friends arrived at a port.
They went to the nearest hotel. They asked what sort of amenities there were. They were told there was a restaurant and a shop.
Across the road there was a supermarket.
They went to the town centre and stopped at the Information office. They asked 'What is there to do here?' They were told that there was a park, a cinema, a theatre, a stadium, a museum and a castle.
They couldn't decide what to do. The first boy wanted to go to the theatre, but the second wanted to go to the cinema.
They started shouting and fighting. The first boy was badly hurt.
Eventually the police arrested them and took them to the police station. One of the boys was taken to hospital.

le port
l'hôtel
le restaurant
le magasin
le supermarché
le centre-ville
Syndicat d'Initiative
le jardin public

le cinéma
le théâtre
le stade
le musée
le château
le commissariat
l'hôpital

There are some groups of nouns that are the same gender and seem to be related to one another. Anecdotes can be used to highlight some of these groups. For instance, the rooms in the house are nearly all feminine. The children are told to imagine Madame Fifi slaving away cleaning all the rooms in the house. Her lazy husband is sitting with his feet up in the sitting-room watching TV or sunning himself in the garden.

This gives us . . .

as opposed to

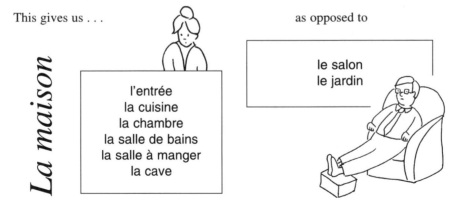

La maison

l'entrée
la cuisine
la chambre
la salle de bains
la salle à manger
la cave

le salon
le jardin

ciLT

Another way of helping children to remember the gender of a group of nouns is to try is to make some sort of controversial statement linking the words of one specific gender.

For instance, out of this long list of animals: *un chien, un cheval, un chat, un oiseau, un poisson, un perroquet, un lion, un serpent, un tigre, un éléphant, un cochon, un cochon d'Inde, un hamster, une tortue, une souris, une araignée, une grenouille, une tarentule,* I declare that I hate all the ones that happen to be in the feminine. Several children will protest, 'But no, I love mice'. Or you could point out little facts like: all the fruits and vegetables that end in an *e* are feminine.

Another very good way of reinforcing the difference between the genders is to encourage the children to use a system of colour-coding the vocabulary: Ask them to write nouns that are feminine in pink or red, and nouns that are masculine in blue or green. You could organise a little competition: Prepare a poster. Group together all the feminine words used, and mount them onto a pink background; do the same with all the masculine words, putting them onto a blue background.

For more able children: Ask them to learn (with correct spellings) between five and ten words a week and test them regularly to ensure the maximum accuracy. Put the list of words to learn during the term into their homework diary.

CONCLUSION

If grammar points can be entertaining and informative at the same time, children are much more likely to remember individual examples. The main issues involved in building an awareness of genders can be summed up as follows:

- In the early stages, introducing the vocabulary in the form of stories in their mother tongue helps them to group nouns of the same gender in their minds. A memory test engages the imagination of the class, and so a concept which is initially unfamiliar to English native speakers becomes much more accessible.

- The repetition of the vocabulary in French by the teacher during the course of the memory game ensures that pupils develop good pronunciation right from the start.

- Verification with a game of '*Pigeon vole*' reinforces the learning process.

- Insisting on a big, or even exaggerated, distinction between the pronunciation of masculine and feminine articles ensures that they store the noun with the correct gender in their mind right from the start.

- Colour-coding when writing down the vocabulary reinforces the distinction.

- For more able children, learning to spell between five and ten words a week will ensure great accuracy in writing.

2.　Building awareness of agreements

One of the hardest and most fundamental aspects of French grammar for English-speaking pupils to grasp is the agreement of adjectives.

This chapter sets out how to go about building up an understanding of a complex grammatical formulation, based on the work programme described in Chapter 1.

INTRODUCING ADJECTIVAL AGREEMENT

Continuity and consistency are important features of an effective approach. Accordingly, the example stories mentioned in Chapter 1 could be used to illustrate both the concept of gender differences and that of subsequent adjective agreements. The class will be familiar with the idea that a story about a little boy will contain masculine nouns, as illustrated previously. A similar principle can be employed to show how agreements work. Once again, if the class can identify a particular object as being from the little boy's story, it will be a masculine noun (prefixed by *un* or *le*), while the feminine nouns in *The little girl's story* will always be prefixed by *une* or *la*.

With frequent repetition and variations on the same story, it will become much easier for everyone in the class to remember which noun 'belongs' to which story and, consequently, determine its gender. Only once the gender of individual nouns is clear is it possible to illustrate how adjectives also agree according to gender.

Conflating the issue of gender with other rules can lead to a degree of complexity that is unnecessary as an introduction to adjectives. For instance, traditional methods for teaching adjective agreements tend to start with words describing colour. This is unfortunate. The grammatical rules which apply to the use of colours are extraordinarily complex.

So instead of starting with colours, I suggest we start with *grand* or *petit*. These words have certain key advantages:

- in the first place there is a very distinct difference in sound between the masculine and feminine forms of these adjectives;

- even more importantly, these two adjectives are placed before the noun both in French and English, and there is no change in the order of the sentence;

- all that is required to make them agree is to add an *e* if the word they describe is feminine.

The technique of using stories to introduce new ideas and vocabulary can just as well be applied in the teaching of adjectives as in the presentation of new nouns. Quite simply, if the word described is from the girl's story, the adjectives will be *grande* or *petite*. The introduction of adjectives here becomes a natural extension of the procedure with which the class has by now become fully familiar. The following example will illustrate the way in which the same method can be applied in this context.

The nouns in the little boy's classroom story should be written in blue or black on the board in a long column. This time, leave a gap between the article and the noun. The same format could be repeated with the feminine nouns found in the little girl's classroom story.

This gives us:

in blue	
un	garçon
un	sac
un	livre
un	cahier
un	crayon
un	stylo
un	ordinateur
un	magnétophone
un	walkman

in red	
une	fille
une	classe
une	porte
une	montre
une	fenêtre
une	chaise
une	trousse
une	règle
une	gomme
une	table
une	calculatrice
une	boîte
une	platine-laser
une	télévision
une	radio

Apart from the space that has been left between the article and the noun, this preparatory phase will be familiar to them. Preparing for the exercise in this way gives the class an extra pointer in deciding on agreements for themselves. From the column above it is easier for children to work out which adjectives must have an *e* added to them in order to agree with particular nouns. This, in turn, helps to build confidence in finding the right answer and trains the mind to think in a correct, grammatical way.

What follows are some helpful classroom exercises and games that you can use to reinforce the notion of gender and lead children gradually to an understanding of this concept.

YOU HAVE BEEN SHRUNK BY A SPACE RAY!

Ask the class to imagine that they have been shrunk by a space ray. They are now very small. All the everyday classroom objects around them are now giant objects: a pen seems much larger, a door enormous, etc.

When describing the things around them, they have to prefix every noun with the adjective *grand* or *grande*: '**un grand** *stylo*', '**un grand** *ordinateur*'; and similarly: '**une grande** *porte*', '**une grande** *table*', if the noun is feminine.

INTRODUCING COLOURS

Only when the class is aware of when to use the masculine and feminine form of the adjective is it appropriate to move on to adjectives of colour. When teaching the words for colours, it is useful to begin the lesson by writing two colour-coded lists on the right-hand side of the board. In one list, all the adjectives to describe colour should appear in the masculine form in blue, and in the other, all the feminine adjectives should be written in red.

The class has to be made aware of several key rules which are new for an English speaker, before they can begin to use these words correctly. This list gives some indication of how quickly things can get complicated:

- the adjective describing colour goes after the noun, rather than before it;

- if the noun appears in the little girl's story and is therefore feminine, an *e* must be added to the adjective to make it agree;

- if the word for a particular colour ends with an *e*, there is no need to add an *e*;

- if, like *blanc*, it ends with a *c*, *h* and *e* should be added;

- if the word derives from a word for a fruit, no agreement is needed, e.g. *marron, abricot, pêche, orange*;

- if the word derives from a word of a metal, no agreement is needed, e.g. *or, argent*.

Having introduced the idea that adjectives agree with the noun they describe, the general rules governing where to put the adjective in a sentence can be illustrated by talking about the colours of various objects in the classroom.

The fact that there are so many rules surrounding the use of adjectives of colour in French can seem daunting at first, so it is important to allow plenty of time for them to become clear to everyone. Again, there is no substitute for a wide range of different examples that can illustrate these rules in a clear and memorable way. The key here is to build up the rules gradually, using exercises that deal with one particular aspect at a time.

Alert the children to the fact that many adjectives in French are placed after the noun in a sentence. Despite exceptions such as *grand* and *petit* mentioned above, the position of adjectives in a sentence in French is not usually the same as in English. This difference should not be ignored. It has to be explained by acknowledging how strange it is for English native speakers to see sentences in which the adjective comes after the noun, as is often the case in French. The whole class then take it in turn to construct **in English** at least three sentences in this way, saying the object first, followed by its colour: a ruler yellow, a chair green, a door white and so on.

The world has turned red!

The same exercise can then be repeated **in French**, using only one colour, *rouge*, to describe everything children see around them in the classroom, as if the world had turned red!

un ordinateur rouge   *une porte rouge*

The world has turned green!

Having made sure that everyone has genuinely understood, the same exercise is repeated. This time the world has turned green. The principle is the same, although an *e* would be added if the object is in *The little girl's story*, just like in the *grand* or *petit* exercise, or in the game *You have been shrunk by a space ray*. Exaggerate the pronunciation of the article *une* and the ending *e* of *verte*.

(Note: it is better at this point to avoid using colours *marron, pêche, orange,* or *argent,* as they are invariable adjectives.)

BUILDING LINGUISTIC CONFIDENCE

The method described above is designed as a gradual introduction to the notion of agreements of adjectives, particularly of adjectives of colour. Instead of introducing all the grammatical rules immediately, which would seem daunting to a class of first-time language learners, the approach favoured here is a gradual building-up of steps which combine to illustrate the particular nuances of agreement in adjectives.

- The memory game for gender distinction
- When to add an *e* — the *You have been shrunk by a space ray* game for gender agreement
- *The world has turned red* game for position
- *The world has turned green* game for position and agreement

The lists of nouns and adjectives suggested in this method can be adapted to illustrate increasingly complex tasks. It is useful to have ready-prepared lists of nouns and adjectives (colour-coded as masculine and feminine) available for each new game.

Using lists of nouns and adjectives in this way will prove invaluable when children start to build up a more complicated sentence in which more than one adjective refers to a particular noun. Having the words on the board in colour-coded tables makes the process of deciding on the position and necessary agreement of the adjective much easier to work out, and leads to a gradual understanding of this new concept.

If the class is familiar with the position of different adjectives in a sentence (such as before the noun for *grand* and *petit*, and after the noun for colours), this will greatly facilitate the construction of compound descriptions later, such as: *un grand livre vert, une petite table blanche, mon adorable petit chat blanc.*

It is never sufficient simply to set out rules. They need to be reinforced in a variety of different ways. The following games help to drive the message home.

UNE AUTOMOBILE

This is a well-known French counting game used, like '*Eeny, meeny, miney, mo*', to determine who will start first.

*U*ne automobile,

Roule, roule, roule,

Où va-t-elle s'arrêter?

En . . .

France	Angleterre	Suisse
Allemagne	Belgique	Espagne
Italie	*Russie*	Australie
Amérique	Chine	Hollande
Irlande	Écosse	Inde
Australie	Iran	Israel
Egypte	Grèce	

De quelle couleur est . . ?

rouge	jaune	mauve
rose	brune	verte
grise	noire	bleue
blanche		

As-tu du . . . sur toi?

rouge	jaune	mauve
rose	brun	vert
gris	noir	bleu
blanc		

 Oui!
Bravo, tu gagnes!

 Non!
Je recommence!

Children stand in a circle. They all chant together '*Une automobile*', etc. With each syllable, everyone points in unison to one child after another. When they get to '*s'arrêter . . .*' they stop. The child they are pointing to has to name a country from the list. Working through the list, they point, going round the circle as before, until they get to the named country. This time the child they are pointing to chooses a colour. The game continues until they reach the chosen colour. The child they are pointing to wins if he or she is wearing something of the same colour.

CILT

For example:

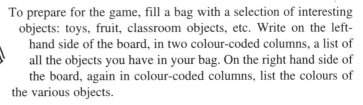

Une automobile,	Verte.
Roule, roule, roule,	As-tu du vert sur toi?
Où va-t-elle s'arrêter?	Oui . . .
En Allemagne.	Tu gagnes!
De quelle couleur est	
l'Allemagne?	

QU'EST-CE QUE J'AI DANS CE PAQUET?

To prepare for the game, fill a bag with a selection of interesting objects: toys, fruit, classroom objects, etc. Write on the left-hand side of the board, in two colour-coded columns, a list of all the objects you have in your bag. On the right hand side of the board, again in colour-coded columns, list the colours of the various objects.

Give the children a piece of paper each and ask them to make an inventory of all the objects you have pulled out. Each object must be written down with the correct article *un* or *une* and with its colour in the form agreeing with the noun — and each colour must be in its proper position, after the noun. The winner is the child with the longest, accurate list.

The main rule of the game is that if the noun is in the red column (feminine), the colour should be taken from the corresponding red adjective column (feminine) and placed after the noun. Similarly, if the noun is in the blue column (masculine), the colour must be taken from the blue column (masculine) and placed after the noun. The person with the longest accurate list of objects and colours wins the game.

UN JEU DE MÉMOIRE

This game works on a similar principle as the one above, although in this instance, the children have to try to remember what they have seen, and select the corresponding French word from a list of vocabulary on the board.

Divide the class into several teams. Pile a tray high with interesting objects. Write the word for each object on the board, in colour-coded lists as before. Hold up the objects one at a time, so that everyone can hear how to pronounce the French equivalent, and can remember its colour. Cover the tray.

Give each child a piece of paper and ask them to write down a list of all the objects that they can remember and the colour of each one. Each object must be written down with the correct article *un* or *une* and with its colour in the form agreeing with the noun — and each colour must be in its proper position, after the noun, as before. The winner is the child with the longest accurate list.

Again, the game is simplified by using the colour-coded lists on the board. In this way, even if a child forgets the gender of a particular object, he or she can still make the adjective agree by working out which column it falls into on the board.

LES VÊTEMENTS

For this game you will need two dials. To make these, cut out two hexagons from thick card, and put a matchstick in the centre of each one to act as a pivot. Before the class, prepare the dials by drawing and colouring a different article of clothing on each section of the hexagon. Use a white shirt, a yellow skirt, etc or choose other similar examples.

On a piece of A4 paper draw a boy and a girl. Each one must be wearing six out of the twelve articles of clothing on the dials. Photocopy the pictures, so that there are enough drawings for everyone in the class to choose whether they would prefer to dress a boy or a girl. Divide the class into teams.

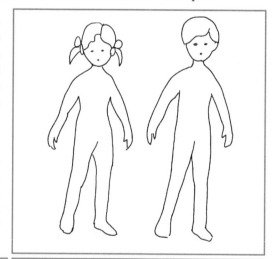

Children take it in turns to spin both dials and, according to the pictures on them, colour in the corresponding items on their own drawings. Each child can colour in the picture only if the item appears on the dial, and if it has not already been coloured in on his or her drawing.

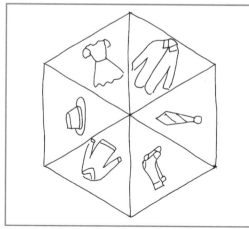

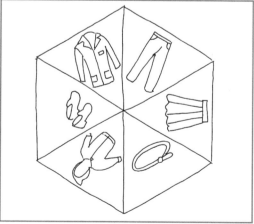

cilt

So, for example, if a child picks the drawing of a boy and the dials are spun to reveal *un pantalon* and *une jupe,* he or she can colour in the trousers (if these are still left to colour). Each time, the child who has spun should construct a simple sentence to describe the new item his or her drawing is wearing:

'*Il/Elle porte une chemise blanche et des chaussures noires.*'

The game can be adapted for a more advanced class, so that children write each item and sentence down, rather than simply constructing their sentences orally.

The game itself is based on the principle of Bingo. The first child to colour and say all six articles of clothing correctly wins the game. The element of competition increases concentration and stimulates interest once more.

> To increase the sense of urgency, encourage the class to use phrases like:
>
> '*C'est mon tour*'
> '*C'est ton tour*'
> '*C'est son tour*'
> '*Allons, vite*'
> '*Dépêche-toi!*'

LE SUPER-CHAMPION DE LA CLASSE!

This is another version of the memory games introduced above. Ideally, children should be sitting in a circle in order to play the game, so that everyone can see everyone else. Give each child a flash card with a coloured picture of an animal, a fruit, or an object on it. Ask everyone to hold their cards so that they can be seen clearly.

One child begins the game by naming the object on his flash card, with its colour. The second child repeats what the first said, and adds his or her own coloured object to the list. This continues around the circle, with each child adding another object to the growing list.

If a child makes a mistake, or hesitates too much, he or she is out of the game, but must still hold the card up for the others to see. The winner is the one who can name all the flash cards correctly, without hesitation. *Le super-champion* is the one who can name all the cards from memory with his or her back to the class!

LES JOUETS EN PELUCHE

Ask the children to bring their favourite soft toy into school. Write a colour-coded list of all the toys on the board (blue and red for masculine and feminine nouns again).

For example:

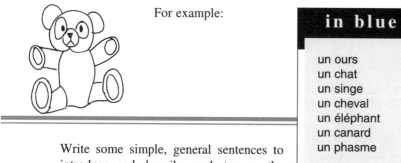

in blue	in red
un ours	une tortue
un chat	une grenouille
un singe	une souris
un cheval	une araignée
un éléphant	une girafe
un canard	une poule
un phasme	une tarentule

Write some simple, general sentences to introduce and describe each toy on the board:

in blue	in red
C'est un . . .	C'est une . . .
Il s'appelle . . .	Elle s'appelle . . .
Il a . . . ans.	Elle a . . . ans.
Il est beau/ mIgnon/ adorable/horrible/ méchant	Elle est belle/ mignonne/adorable/ horrible/ méchante

Ask each child in turn to come to the front of the class to introduce his or her favourite toy to everyone, practising the agreements of the adjectives, depending on whether the toy is gendered masculine or feminine.

LES MIMES

Mime games provide one of the most effective methods of encouraging children to participate in practice exercises. Often those who are very shy and reluctant to speak in class are the ones to excel in this activity.

Write a list of about ten different adjectives referring to moods and emotions on the board, using colour-coded columns to highlight differences between masculine and feminine agreements.

The same adjectives should be written on ready-prepared cards, to be picked by each child in turn.

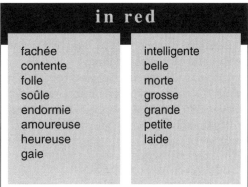

in blue		in red	
fâché	intelligent	fachée	intelligente
content	beau	contente	belle
fou	mort	folle	morte
soûl	gros	soûle	grosse
endormi	grand	endormie	grande
amoureux	petit	amoureuse	petite
heureux	laid	heureuse	laide
gai		gaie	

For example the card could read:

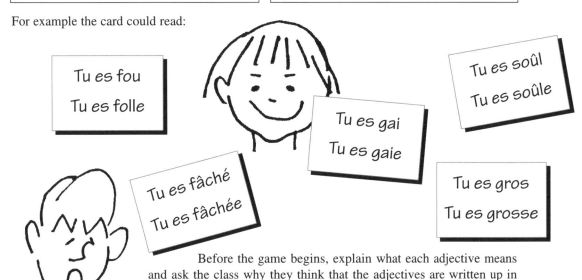

Before the game begins, explain what each adjective means and ask the class why they think that the adjectives are written up in two separate columns on the board. One child picks a card and mimes the mood to the others, who try to guess which mood is being expressed, saying, for example: '*Il est fâché*' or '*Elle est fâchée*'. If they guess correctly, the child miming answers: '*Oui, je suis fâché/e*'. The game continues until each member of the class has had a turn at miming a mood for the others to guess.

Once the class is familiar with the game, and with the emotions mimed, the same format can be taken one step further to include descriptions of how several people feel at once. This introduces the differences between *Ils* and *Elles* and shows how adjectives also agree in the plural. It is important to explain that *Il* and *Elle* like 'He' and 'She' become 'They'.

THE FRENCH POSSESSIVE ADJECTIVES

The easiest, clearest way to introduce possessive adjectives is with a description of families. Make sure that when children learn the words for 'mother', 'father', etc they are always accompanied by the relevant possessive adjective. So, the example will always be **ma mère, mon père, mon frère**, etc. Explain that *ma* is for the female relations, and *mon* for the masculine relations, so that they can imagine each member of their own families as they learn the relevant words. Imagining real people to fit the descriptions makes the difference between *mon* and *ma* seem much clearer.

If a child uses the wrong possessive adjective with the noun — for example, if someone says '*ma frère*' by mistake, joke, 'Oh! so is your brother a girl now?', to make the distinction between masculine and feminine more immediate.

(Incidentally, an easy way to remember the direction of the accent of the words *père, mère, frère, grand-père,* is to suggest that they can salute their family with their right hand, as a mark of respect, and the accent will always go the same way.)

Once the differences between *mon, ma* and *mes* have been understood and practised, the same principles for *ton, ta, tes* and *son, sa, ses* are easy to grasp.

Steven Fawkes, in Pathfinder 25: *With a song in my scheme of work*, offers an easy way of remembering possessive adjectives, by adapting the tune of '*Frère Jacques*'. Again, the tune is familiar, as is the notion of introducing new grammar concepts via songs, as in previous examples, and the song ensures that the points introduced are more easily remembered.

mon	ma	mes
ton	ta	tes
son	sa	ses
notre	notre	nos
votre	votre	vos
leur	leur	leurs
le	la	les

mon ma mes...

COMPARISONS — THE SUPERLATIVE

Give each child a sheet of paper. Ask them to fold it in two lengthways and in four widthways. Tell them to write *PLUS* in large capital letters in the first rectangle, *MOINS*, in the second, and then *GRAND, GRANDE, BEAU, BELLE, AUSSI* and *STUPIDE* in the remaining spaces. Ask them to cut out their paper, so that they each have eight 'papers' in front of them.

PLAY YOUR CARDS RIGHT

Using:

Divide the class in small teams for the game of *Play your cards right!* Shuffle a pack of playing cards and show the whole class the first card, then ask: '*La prochaine carte sera plus ou moins grande?*'

Each member of the team has to decide whether the next card will be higher or lower than the card they have just seen. They should then hold

In their left hand: In their right hand:

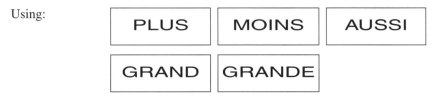

Explain that for this game, they will need the card marked *GRANDE* as the word for a card is '***une** carte*'.

When the second card is turned over and shown to the class, the members of the team which has predicted either higher or lower correctly win a point. The game is then repeated several times and the winners are members of the team with the most correct predictions, and so the greatest number of points, at the end of the game.

Using:

Prepare a bag full of interesting objects. Write a list of words for the objects on the board, using colour-coded columns for masculine and feminine nouns again. Stand at the front of the class, and pull two objects of different sizes from the bag at once. The class should decide which of the two objects is larger.

In their left hands, they should hold up the cards marked either *PLUS, MOINS* or *AUSSI*, depending on whether the first of the two objects is larger, smaller, or the same size as the second one. In their right hands, they should choose and hold up the card marked *GRAND*, if the first object is masculine in gender, and *GRANDE* if it is feminine. Each child who manages to choose correctly between both *PLUS, MOINS, AUSSI*, and *GRAND* and *GRANDE* is awarded a point for their team.

A VOUS LE VOTE! VOTEZ VITE!

Using:
MOINS	PLUS	AUSSI	BEAU	BELLE

This game encourages the class to combine the adjectives in order to judge which is the more or less attractive of two images.

Cut a selection of pictures from magazines and hold them up to the class two at a time. Each child then compares the first image to the second image and decides which of the two is more attractive. By holding up a combination of cards he or she casts his or her vote.

When asking them to compare, you could name the person in the first picture and ask: '. . . *est plus ou moins beau/belle que* . . ?' — here naming the person in the second picture.

Using only two of the five cut-out rectangles, the children can cast their vote. They must hold up either *PLUS, MOINS* or *AUSSI* in one hand, and *BEAU* or *BELLE* in the other hand, depending on whether the first picture of the two is of a man or a woman. Award one point for each accurate answer. Repeat the exercise with different pictures.

A vous le vote!

VRAI OU FAUX?

Give two cards one marked *VRAI* and one marked *FAUX* to everyone in the class. The

VRAI	or	FAUX

children have to decide whether the different statements they hear are true or false, *VRAI* or *FAUX*, by holding up either one of the cards.

CiLT

PORTRAITS: 1

On the board, prepare colour-coded tables of words for describing people's bodies, and a list of adjectives and jobs, also colour-coded for masculine and feminine.

Each child should invent and write down a description of a person in the school. The description is read out and the children must guess who the writer had in mind. Award two points if the description is good enough for the class to guess who is being described, and award an extra point for accurate agreements!

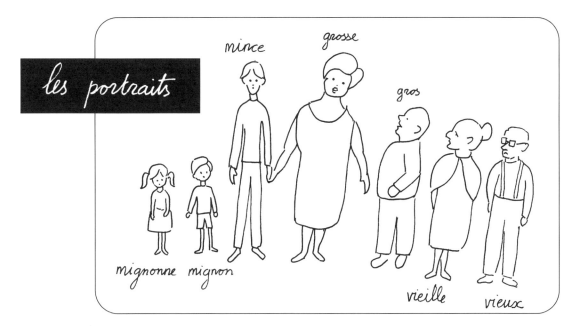

PORTRAITS: 2

This is a particularly useful game to revise all previous vocabulary. Write some colour-coded questions on the board to guide the class through the exercise.

in blue

Est-ce que c'est un garçon/un homme?
Est-ce qu'il a les yeux bleus?
Est-ce qu'il a un grand nez?
Est-ce qu' il est beau?
Est-ce qu'il porte un T-shirt noir?
C'est un danseur/un footballeur/
un politicien?

in red

Est-ce que c'est une fille/une femme?
Est-ce qu'elle a de longs cheveux?
Est-ce qu'elle est grosse?
Est-ce qu'elle porte une jupe verte?
Est-ce qu'elle est intelligente?
C'est une chanteuse/une actrice/
une musicienne?

Ask everyone to bring in some pictures of famous people, cut out from magazines or newspapers. With the help of the class choose around ten pictures from the selection, asking: *'Celui-ci?'* *'Non!'* *'Celle-là?'* *'Oui!'* *'D'accord'*.

Stick them onto the board with Blu-tack. Next, go round the class, asking, *'Comment s'appelle-t-elle'* or *'s'appelle-t-il?'* to ensure that they know all the names of all the celebrities pictured.

Ask one volunteer to leave the room. Choose one of the celebrities from the board, and when the volunteer comes back in, he or she can ask a maximum of five questions to try to determine which celebrity was chosen. After five questions, the volunteer must guess who they think was picked, asking: *'C'est . . ?'*, to which the class can all shout *'Oui!'* or *'Non!'*

BUILDING A RESOURCE BANK

Build up a resources bank of little cards, of all the sentences or phrases the children have come across during the various exercises suggested above.

Keep them close at hand, to use between activities. Alternatively, encourage the children to finish quickly to play some additional games writing down, rather than shouting out, their answers.

You can gradually build up your resource bank as you try more and more exercises and variations, depending on how different classes respond to the suggestions made here. Mark on individual cards each phrase or sentence they refer to, and which agreements have been tackled. Number them and use them whenever there are a few minutes to spare.

For example, the following sentences could be translated into French:

A white rubber	My little white mouse.	He is small.
I have a green pencil.	His dog is naughty.	Look at my white cats.
I like a small cat.	My little sister is cute.	I have six green pencils.
My big green books.	I would like a blue T-shirt.	He is bigger than Tom
Mireille is intelligent.	Your dress is pretty.	
I am stupid!	She is drunk!	

CONCLUSION

By structuring a programme of games and activities, confidence can be built effectively. Adjectival agreement need not be over-complicated for children to learn, so long as the approach is gradual, rigorous and fun.

3. Introducing plurals

Once the idea of agreement has been firmly established, the plural can be introduced with confidence.

Unlike agreements of gender, the idea of the plural form of the French nouns should not prove too complicated since both languages mark the difference between the singular and the plural in most cases with an *s*. The only difference between the two languages is that the *s* is not pronounced in French.

The easiest way to introduce this is by using lots of examples, both oral and written, until the class becomes familiar with the idea. As with everything else, practice makes perfect!

'SUR LE PONT D'AVIGNON'

You can find the tune of this very popular song on the cassette *Le français par le chant* by Dominique Field and Margot Forbes. The children hold hands and dance in a circle. When they get to '*Les messieurs font comme ça*' they stop and bow politely. '*Et puis encore comme ça*', they bow again. They then hold hands and start chanting but they must substitute '*les messieurs. . .*' with a different group of people. For example: '*Les dames font comme ça*', they nod politely. '*Les demoiselles font comme ça*', they curtsy. '*Les musiciens font . . .*', they can improvise and, for instance, pretend to play the piano or the violin, etc.

Sur le pont d'Avignon	Les dames	
On y danse, on y danse,	Les demoiselles	
Sur le pont d'Avignon,	Les musiciens	
On y danse tout en rond.	Les danseurs	
	Les professeurs	
Les demoiselles font comme ça.	Les gangsters	Les acrobates
Et puis encore comme ça.	Les artistes	Les médecins
		Les juges
Sur le pont d'Avignon		Les footballers
On y danse, on y danse,		Les bébés
Sur le pont d'Avignon,		Les garçons
On y danse tout en rond.		Les filles

This little merry-go-round provides a very easy way of introducing the vocabulary for different occupations. Draw their attention to the fact that in French the *s* and *x* of the plural are silent.

'SAVEZ-VOUS PLANTER LES CHOUX?'

This is a very well-known French merry-go-round. You can find the tune in *A la page no. 1* by Denis Grayson. Children hold hands and sing:

Savez-vous planter les choux, à la mode, à la mode, Savez-vous planter les choux, à la mode de chez nous? On les plante avec les pieds, à la mode, à la mode, On les plante avec les pieds, à la mode de chez nous.	Les jambes Les bras Les coudes Les mains Les doigts Les oreilles Les yeux Les fesses Les genoux

Each time they mention a different part of the body, they mime the action accordingly. As you introduce the new vocabulary, draw their attention again to the fact that the final *s* and *x* that mark the plural are silent.

The children hold hands and dance in a circle. When they get to: '*On les plante avec les . . .*' they must name a part of the body and mime the action of using this part of the body to plant the cabbages. This game is very popular with young children.

AGREEMENTS OF ADJECTIVES

LES BANANES

In the cassette *Zozo French party* by Teresa Scibor, there is a song that is sung to the tune of *Frère Jacques* but the words have been changed.

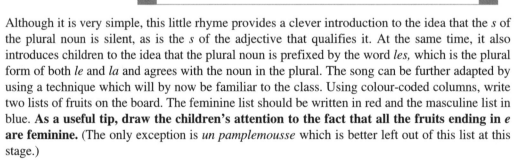

Les bananes
Les bananes
J'adore ça!
Les bananes sont bonnes
Les bananes sont bonnes
Un, deux, trois
Une pour moi!

Although it is very simple, this little rhyme provides a clever introduction to the idea that the *s* of the plural noun is silent, as is the *s* of the adjective that qualifies it. At the same time, it also introduces children to the idea that the plural noun is prefixed by the word *les*, which is the plural form of both *le* and *la* and agrees with the noun in the plural. The song can be further adapted by using a technique which will by now be familiar to the class. Using colour-coded columns, write two lists of fruits on the board. The feminine list should be written in red and the masculine list in blue. **As a useful tip, draw the children's attention to the fact that all the fruits ending in *e* are feminine.** (The only exception is *un pamplemousse* which is better left out of this list at this stage.)

Ask them to write their own little song, like the one above, changing the noun *bananes* for their favourite fruit. Point out the importance of adding an *s* to the fruit and to *bon* or *bonne* in order

in blue		in red	
le citron	les citrons	la pomme	les pommes
le melon	les melons	la banane	les bananes
l' abricot	les abricots	la poire	les poires
le kiwi	les kiwis	la fraise	les fraises
l'ananas	les ananas	la prune	les prunes
		la cerise	les cerises
		la datte	les dattes
		la mangue	les mangues
		la mandarine	les mandarines
		la figue	les figues
		la pêche	les pêches
		la pastèque	les pastèques
		l'orange	les oranges
est bon	sont bons	est bonne	sont bonnes
Un pour toi		**Une pour toi**	

to form the plural and make the adjective agree. Also explain why *une pour* moi changes to *un pour moi*, if the fruit they have chosen appears in the blue column on the board.

UNE ENQUÊTE

Using the same colour-coded fruit list, go round the class asking: '*Quel est ton fruit préféré?*' They are not allowed to quote more then one type of fruit. They have to answer, for example: '*Je préfère les fraises.*' Point out to them the fact that in English as in French, when we are expressing our likes or dislikes of fruits or animals, we use the plural. We therefore have to add an *s* to the fruit or animal. As we are dealing with a particular group of things we use the definite article: *les*.

Mark on the board the result of your survey. For example:

Les pommes	3	Les poires	2	Les bananes	2	Les oranges	1
Les pastèques	4	Les fraises	5	Les cerises	2	Les abricots	1

Ask the children to register this information on a pie chart, '*UN DIAGRAMME CIRCULAIRE*' sometimes called '*CAMEMBERT!*' Draw a large circle on a piece of paper. Divide it as evenly as possible in as many segments as there are children in the classroom. Photocopy it and give one to every child. They have to write down the list of fruits in the plural and to mark the colour key they will use next to it. They then have to colour the different segments accordingly.

'*DIAGRAMME EN BARRES*': give a piece of squared paper to each child and show them how to register the result of their *enquête* with a bar chart. Stress the importance of writing the fruits in the plural in the key.

UN DÉFILÉ DE MODE

Ask each child to provide a picture of an item of clothing. They can either draw the item, or find a picture in a magazine and cut it out. Write down the vocabulary for each item in two colour-coded columns on the board, and **draw the children's attention to the fact that some words, like *pantalon, jean* and *short*, are singular in French, although in English we are used to them being in the plural.**

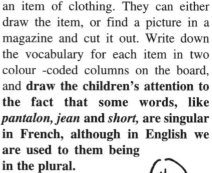

On the right hand side of the board, write the colours in two colour-coded columns for masculine and feminine. It is better to avoid at this stage colours such as *marron* or *or*. To the list on the right hand side of the board, you can add *à rayures* and *à pois*.

CILT

in blue	in red	in blue	in red
un short	une veste	rouge	rouge
un jean	une robe	jaune	jaune
un pantalon	une jupe	orange	orange
un T-shirt	une cravate	mauve	mauve
un sweatshirt	une écharpe	rose	rose
un pull		vert	verte
un anorak		bleu	bleue
un chapeau		noir	noire
un manteau		gris	grise
un imperméable		blanc	blanche
des baskets	des chaussures	_____ s	_____ s
	des chaussettes	_____ s	_____ s
	des bottes	_____ s	_____ s

Stick the new collection on the board with Blu-tack. Each child should have a turn to present the fashion show. As presenter, (*le présentateur/la présentatrice*) they pick a selection of their favourite items and describe them to the class on a tape recorder.

The rest of the class assumes the role of the press (*les journalistes*), writing down the details of five items of their choice.

If the game is played with a more advanced class, they could add comments such as: *C'est super! C'est chic! C'est moderne! C'est élégant! C'est chouette! C'est moche! J'aime ça! Je n'aime pas ça!*

LES MONSTRES

Plurals relate to numbers, and numbers can be fun, especially when they are random. One game that draws on the surprise factor involved in randomness is this monster game. For this game you will need three hexagonal dials. Write the different parts of the body on two of the dials, and on the other one put different colours (see following page).

Divide the class into teams of four. Give a piece of paper to each child. Give a set of spinners and some felt pens or colouring pencils to each group. Each child takes it in turn to spin the three spinners. The idea is to make monsters. One of the spinners must stop on *la tête* for a team to start their drawings. From then on the rest of the drawing is added according to the outcome of the three dials.

la tête	l'œil	jaune
la bouche	le nez	rouge
la jambe	le corps	vert
la main	le bras	bleu
l'oreille	le pied	blanc
l'antenne	les cheveux	noir

The monster must have at least one of everything. The children must write a description of their monster. Remind the children that unlike other nouns, the word for eye changes completely in the plural — *œil* becomes *yeux* — and that *nez* and *bras* don't need an *s* in the plural. For example:

> *Mon monstre a deux têtes rouges et une tête bleue.*
> *Une queue noire. Deux pieds bleus. Deux pieds jaunes.*
> *Quatre yeux verts. Une bouche jaune.* etc.

The winner is the one in the group that has a complete monster and an accurate description. Special care should be given to agreements of the plurals.

The children should be encouraged to speak in French throughout the game: *'C'est mon tour.'* *'C'est ton tour.'* *'Vite.'* *'Passe-moi les feutres.'* *'Joue.'* *'Dessine.'* *'Colorie.'* *'Je gagne.'* *'C'est chouette!'*

COMPETITIONS

Competitions are a great incentive to follow instructions and do well. You don't need to have expensive prizes. Just a commendation card is sufficient to motivate the class.

L'EXTRA-TERRESTRE

To complement the last game and add an appealingly creative dimension, the class can be encouraged to generate hilarious plurals for themselves.

Write a list of vocabulary describing bodies and faces on the board, in four colour-coded columns, this time one for the masculine, one for the masculine plural, one for the feminine and one for the feminine plural.

in blue			in red	
un œil	des yeux		une bouche	des bouches
un nez	des nez		une oreille	des oreilles
un cheveu	des cheveux		une main	des mains
un cou	des cous		une jambe	des jambes
un bras	des bras		une antenne	des antennes
un ventre	des ventres		une queue	des queues
un pied	des pieds		une aile	des ailes

Ask the children to draw an extra-terrestrial with as many heads, arms, eyes, etc as they like. Get them to write down in French how many of each feature their extra-terrestrial has.

Remind them that if the extra-terrestrial has more than one of any feature (more than one head for example), the noun must be written in the plural. Ask them again to pay particular attention to the fact that, unlike other nouns, the word for eye changes completely in the plural. *Œil* becomes *yeux, nez* and *bras* don't need an *s* in the plural, *cheveu* ends with a silent *x* in the plural.

Once the class has finished, stick all the drawings on the board with Blu-tack. Give each child three 'Post-it' stickers. Write on the first: *Premier prix*, on the second: *Deuxième prix* and on the third: *Troisième prix*.

They must come to the board in groups of four and stick up their stickers independently and silently to cast their votes. They are not allowed to vote for their own drawing.

LE GRAND DESSINATEUR DE MODE

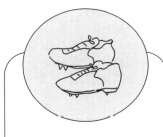

Draw and label an outfit for your favourite football club.

Write down a small description.

Take special care of agreements of adjectives.

Draw and label an outfit for the latest pop group.

Write down a small description

Take special care with the agreements of adjectives.

Draw and label a school uniform.

Write down a small description.

Take special care with the agreements of adjectives.

This competition is to be judged by all the class.

A VOUS LE VOTE!

Stick all the new creations on the board with Blu-tack. Give every child three 'Post-it' stickers. Write on the first: *Premier prix*, on the second: *Deuxième prix* and on the third: *Troisième prix*.

Ask the children to come to the board in groups of four and quickly stick up their stickers to cast their vote. They are not allowed to vote for their own drawing!

You could vary what is written on the 'Post-it' stickers: *'C'est super!' 'C'est beau!' 'C'est chic!' 'C'est élégant!' 'C'est moche!' 'C'est laid!' 'C'est affreux!' 'C'est drôle!'*

INTRODUCING *C'EST . . .* AND *CE SONT . . .*

BLOCKBUSTER

If you have an overhead projector, start by photocopying the grid below on a transparency.

Prepare different shaped counters to represent each team. Ten of each should be sufficient.

The counters must be smaller than the hexagons of the grid as you will place them on the transparency each time a team scores. Your counters could be in the shape of:

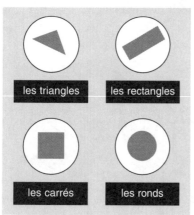

les triangles

les rectangles

les carrés

les ronds

or:

les voitures   les avions   les bateaux   les vélos

This game is based on a popular TV show.

The aim of the game is to get from one side of the grid to the other in an uninterrupted line by answering questions correctly and placing a counter on the corresponding hexagon. The team that gets an uninterrupted line wins.

CiLT

Divide the class into four teams. Each member of the first team plays, in turn, against each member of the second team. The other teams then play against each other in the same way. At the end of the matches, the winning teams play in the final. To put a counter on a hexagon, children have to create a phrase correctly, without conferring or prompting, by following the instructions you give. **Each member of the team answers one question at a time and then his opponent gets a go to try to block him.**

Before the game starts, explain the rules. **At first keep the rules very simple to build their confidence.** Give examples on the way you would like them to give you their answer. For instance you might want them to identify a picture. Decide if they need to emphasise the gender with the definite or indefinite article or the possessive adjective, or for a more advanced class by forming a complete sentence.

Mon, ma or *mes:* ask them to identify the picture by using the possessive adjectives. Like all adjectives in French the possessive adjectives have endings which must correspond to the nouns they relate to. For example they can be asked to say : '*Mon chien*', '*Mes poissons*', or '*Ma tortue*'.

Son, sa or *ses:*	*Son chien*	*Ses poissons*	*Sa tortue*
Notre or *nos:*	*Notre chien*	*Nos poissons*	*Nos Tortues*

'*C'est . . .* ' or '*Ce sont . . .*': '*C'est un chat*'. If a hexagon has more than one animal they must say '*Ce sont des chats*'.

'*Les*' and '*des*': once they have understood the game, you can make the rules a bit more difficult by asking them to add '*Ce sont des tortues. J'aime les tortues!/Je n'aime pas les tortues!*' according to their likes or dislikes. **This exercise will stress the difference between *des* and *les*.**

The beauty of the game is that it can be adapted to cover all sorts of vocabulary.

ARTICLES: SINGULAR AND PLURAL

For this game the children should know how to pronounce the French alphabet correctly. You can use the tune of 'When the saints come marching in' to teach them or you can improvise your own tune.

UN/UNE OR *LE/LA?*

Play a game based on the *I spy* game to make them understand the difference between the definite and indefinite article. Stare at an object and say for example: '*Je regarde quelque chose qui commence avec . . .*' name the first letter of the word, for example '*C*'.

They have to follow your gaze and then have a guess. '*C'est le cahier?*' '*Non!*' '*C'est le crayon?*' '*Oui!*'. Because they are referring to a specific object they can see, they must use the definite article.

When you say '*Je pense à quelque chose qui commence avec C*', they have to find out which category the word is in by asking:

C'est *un animal?*	*un vêtement?*	*un objet?*
un fruit ?	*un légume?*	*un dessert?* *une boisson?*

Once they have established which category it is in, they have a guess and answer using the indefinite article *un/une*. '*C'est un animal?*' '*Oui!*' '*C'est un chat?*' '*Non!*' '*C'est un chien?*' '*Non!*' '*C'est un cheval?*' '*Oui!*'.

LES OR DES?

Building on children's understanding of this game, the next stage is to introduce articles in the plural. The game can be repeated, substituting *une chose* by *des choses*.

For example: '*Je regarde des choses qui commencent avec C.*' '*Ce sont **les** cahiers?*' '*Non!*' '*Ce sont **les** crayons?*' '*Oui!*' Because you are looking at these particular things they have to use the definite article *les*.

'*Je pense à des choses qui commencent avec C.*' They have to find out which category the objects belongs to:

Ce sont des objets?	*des vêtements?*	*des fruits?*
des légumes?	*des desserts?*	*des boissons?*

They then have a guess using the indefinite article *des*. '*Ce sont des vêtements?*' '*Non!*' '*Ce sont **des** fruits?*' '*Non!*' '*Ce sont **des** légumes?*' '*Oui!*' '*Ce sont **des** carottes?*' '*Non!*' '*Ce sont **des** choux?*' '*Oui!*'

QUEL EST MON MÉTIER?

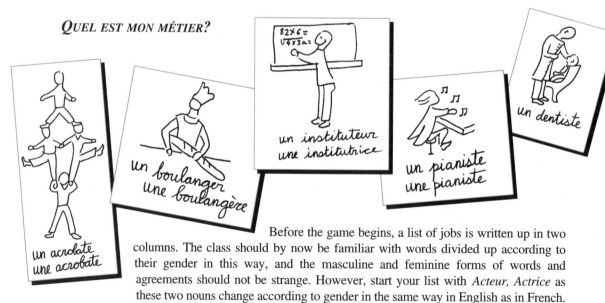

Before the game begins, a list of jobs is written up in two columns. The class should by now be familiar with words divided up according to their gender in this way, and the masculine and feminine forms of words and agreements should not be strange. However, start your list with *Acteur, Actrice* as these two nouns change according to gender in the same way in English as in French.

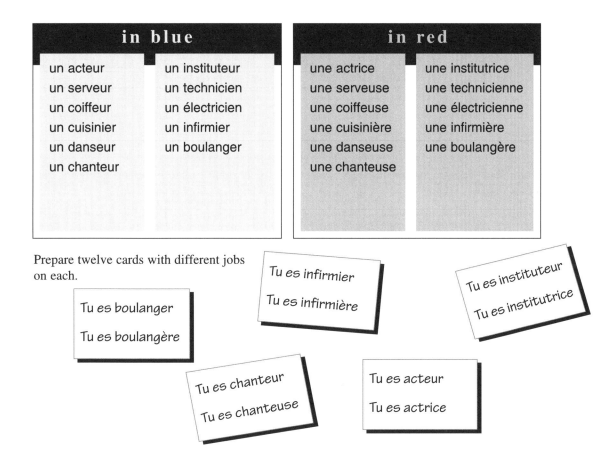

in blue		in red	
un acteur	un instituteur	une actrice	une institutrice
un serveur	un technicien	une serveuse	une technicienne
un coiffeur	un électricien	une coiffeuse	une électricienne
un cuisinier	un infirmier	une cuisinière	une infirmière
un danseur	un boulanger	une danseuse	une boulangère
un chanteur		une chanteuse	

Prepare twelve cards with different jobs on each.

Tu es boulanger
Tu es boulangère

Tu es infirmier
Tu es infirmière

Tu es instituteur
Tu es institutrice

Tu es chanteur
Tu es chanteuse

Tu es acteur
Tu es actrice

Each member of the class chooses a card to find their allotted job. They then mime their particular job for the class, which has to guess what it is that they do. Guided by the colour-coded lists of words on the board the class guesses the job by suggesting '*Il est . . ./ elle est . . .*'.

In a further development, several children can be grouped together to mime a particular job. The rest of the class guesses their profession, but substitutes the phrase '*Vous êtes . . .*' for the phrase '*Tu es . . .*' in the first example. Similarly, the group miming answers: '*Oui, nous sommes . . .*' when the class guesses correctly.

Vous êtes cuisiniers.	*Vous êtes coiffeurs.*	*Vous êtes acteurs.*
Vous êtes cuisinières.	*Vous êtes coiffeuses.*	*Vous êtes actrices.*

These exercises introduce the personal pronouns *vous* and *nous*. It is important to stress here that their usual pronunciation is without sounding the *s*. However, since the verb *être* is one early example of a verb which causes this pronunciation to alter, it is helpful to introduce this change by getting the class to think of the *s* bouncing onto the verb *être* and becoming a *z*! So, to obtain the correct pronunciation of the phrase *vous êtes,* the change is illustrated as *vou zêtes.*

Not only are the children now aware of agreements according to gender, but the idea of a plural has been introduced. Over the course of these miming games, the class becomes familiar with new agreements of nouns, verbs and adjectives, and it is important to check that the pronunciation is correct and that these new concepts are properly understood.

CONCLUSION

Once gender and agreement have been established as principles for a class, plurals and the agreements that come with them should present no difficulty. In fact with the similarities between French and English, and the fact that numbers can be fun, this should be a most enjoyable part of the course.

C*i*LT

4.   Prepositions in context

While French does not have the same level of variety and complexity of prepositional uses as English, correct use of prepositions is a fundamental component of fluent and effective mastery of the language. Prepositions can best be introduced by a series of games and exercises which give working examples of how they might function in sentences. Where prepositions are concerned, context is everything. The more memorable and appropriate the context one creates, the better. Before beginning the following exercises, write the prepositions to be covered on the board as a constant reminder for the class. The prepositions should include:

sous, sur, dans, devant, derrière, à côté de, entre

What follows is a selection of games, songs and role plays designed to combine practice with the introduction of new vocabulary.

'LONDON BRIDGE IS FALLING DOWN'

An effective way to introduce new material is via songs which are easily remembered and, once learned, can be adapted to include a variety of vocabulary — for instance, any new words or phrases which need to be practised. Christina Skarbek, in Young Pathfinder 5: *First steps to reading and writing,* provides a working example of this, using the tune of the well-known song 'London Bridge is falling down', to introduce the idea of prepositions. She combines the rhythm of the song with actions that illustrate the meaning of each preposition.

Explain the actions to the class beforehand. By keeping one hand still and moving the other to correspond to each preposition they sing, children have a visual illustration of the significance of each new word. Skarbek's adaptation of the song is as follows:

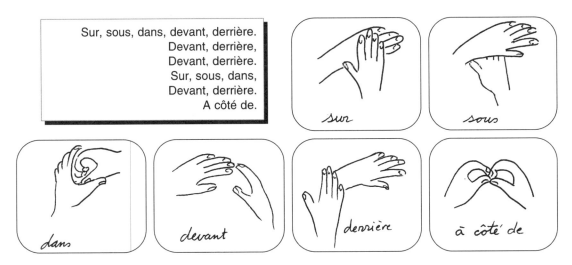

> Sur, sous, dans, devant, derrière.
> Devant, derrière,
> Devant, derrière.
> Sur, sous, dans,
> Devant, derrière.
> A côté de.

This song provides a clear introduction to what each preposition means. Once the class is familiar with the new words, other games can be developed to practise them, ensuring that they are remembered. The element of competition also encourages the class to concentrate more carefully on individual exercises, and promotes accuracy. There follows a series of games and exercises designed to focus specifically on revising and reinforcing the use and particular significance of prepositions.

GAMES

'SIMON DIT . . .' OR 'JACQUES DIT . . .'

The game of *Simon says . . .* can help to illustrate all kinds of new vocabulary, and to supplement the introduction of grammar points, since it is so easily adapted to encompass each new stage of language learning. Here, the vocabulary for classroom objects can be introduced and revised, as well as illustrating the prepositions explained in the song above.

The list of prepositions used should be written on the board as before:

sur	sous	dans	devant	derrière	à côté de	entre

Before the game begins, each child should lay out a collection of classroom objects, such as a pencil, a rubber, a pen, a pencil-case, etc on the desk in front of him or her. Call out 'Simon says . . .' commands for the class to follow, using simple instructions relating to the objects in front of them, such as:

Mets la gomme entre le crayon et la trousse
Mets la règle dans la trousse
Mets le crayon sur ton nez
Regarde à gauche, etc.

The game can be used to practise new words and French sentence construction in an entertaining way. By adapting games such as these, which are already familiar to the class in the context of language learning, children hardly notice that they are repeating vocabulary and points of grammar, and so relax and remember what they learn.

The principle behind the game of *Simon says . . .* can also be developed as a **team game.** Again the exercise involves an understanding of simple sentences which, in turn, allows certain commands to be carried out. As well as revising vocabulary, playing the game in teams encourages greater concentration, while in this format learning through repetition can still be fun.

Arrange four large boxes at the front of the class. Divide the class into four teams, giving each team member a number in French. Call all those with the number *un* to the front of the class, and give them three commands to follow, for example:

CiLT

Mets la boîte sous la table.
Assieds-toi sur la boîte.
Mets-toi à gauche de la boîte.

Award a point for each command correctly carried out.

Next, call all those with the number *deux* to the front of the class, and give them three different commands to follow:

Mets la boîte derrière toi.
Entre dans la boîte.
Mets un crayon devant la boîte.

Again, award a point for each command correctly carried out.

When each number, from each team, has had a turn, add up the points to decide which team has won.

LES STATUES

Another variation of the game of *Simon says . . .* can be played in the playground, if possible. Here, children stand at one end of the playground and you turn your back to them at the other. The game consists of a series of commands in French, which they must follow. The first child to carry them out correctly, and to reach you, wins.

Explain that after executing each command, everyone must stand absolutely still – if anyone moves, they must start again. Turn around after every command to check that no one is moving and that everyone has carried out the command correctly. If anyone moves or laughs, send them back to the beginning.

Here are some examples of orders which could be used:

This game can be played several times, and each time the commands can be varied, until everyone is able to carry out these simple instructions without making mistakes.

Six pas à gauche

Quatre grands pas en avant

Trois pas en avant

Deux grands pas en avant

Cinq pas à droite

Un grand pas en avant

en avant

cilt

CHAUD OU FROID

Back inside the classroom — and using the list of prepositions on the board as before — another useful game to illustrate where objects are positioned is 'Hot and cold', or *'Chaud ou froid'* in French.

| sur | sous | dans | devant | derrière | à côté de | entre | près de |

Here, the class selects an object, for example *un crayon jaune*. While one volunteer is out of the room, another hides the object, describing in French where he or she has put it (*'le crayon jaune est près de la fenêtre'*, for example).

When the volunteer comes back into the classroom, his or her task is to find the object by walking round the room, guided by the rest of the class who say *'froid'* or *'très froid'* if the object is far away, and *'chaud'* or *'très chaud'* the closer the volunteer gets to it.

This game is good to play with beginners, but can also be adapted **for more advanced children.** The principle is the same, but instead of walking around the classroom, the volunteer asks questions to determine where the object has been hidden:

C'est près de Jean?   *C'est près de Marie?*   *C'est sous la chaise de Marie?*
C'est dans le sac de Marie? etc.

The rest of the class answers as before — the volunteer is either *'chaud'* or *'froid'* depending on how close he or she is to discovering where the object is hidden — here the adjectives *'tiède'* and *'brûlant'* can also be used to describe just how near, or far away, the object is:

Froid   Tiède   Chaud   Brûlant

'ATTENTION, OÙ EST . . ?'

This is another variation of the game *Chaud ou froid,* and is one which involves the whole class. This particular example is best played at the beginning of the class and, ideally, the objects to be described should be placed around the classroom before the lesson begins.

The game requires the selection of ten unusual objects — things that would not usually appear in the classroom — which are large enough for everyone to see without leaving their seats. Once they have been positioned around the room, write a list of the objects, and their colours, on the board (in colour-coded columns once more), as follows:

in blue	in red	in blue	in red
un ours un T-shirt un walkman un chat un citron	une poupée une cuillère une fleur une pomme une souris	vert noir gris blanc rouge jaune	verte noire grise blanche rouge jaune

If any of these words are being used for the first time, draw or explain what they mean before the competition begins, so that all the vocabulary is clear.

The list of prepositions should also be written up, as with the previous exercises. It may help to clarify their meaning if they are positioned on the board according to what they signify (*sur* could be written above *sous,* with *dans* in between):

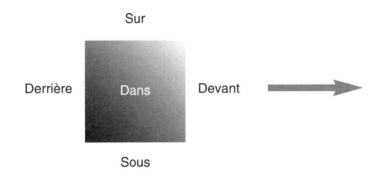

The object of the competition is for the class to identify as many of the unusual objects they see around them as possible, and to describe their position in the classroom by constructing simple sentences, using the vocabulary and prepositions that should, by now, be familiar.

Their sentences should be as follows:

L'ours est sur la fenêtre.   *La fleur est dans la poubelle.*
L'écharpe est devant le tableau.   *Le T-shirt est sous la chaise de Mr Jones.*
L'ours est entre le livre et la montre.   *La pomme est devant la porte,* etc.

The first group of children to spot all the objects, and to describe their positions in the classroom correctly, wins the game.

ATTENTION! CE N'EST PAS À SA PLACE!

Ask a volunteer to look at all the objects in the classroom, and to try to remember where everything is. When he or she has left the room, rearrange some of the more obvious objects.

For example: Put his or her bag in the wastepaper basket.
                 Put a book on his or her chair.
                 Add a desk in a row.
                 Ask a child to change seat.
                 Ask a child to sit on the floor, etc.

When the volunteer comes back in, he or she must try to spot four of the changes you have made, and describe where things have been moved to — using the correct French preposition in each case.

BEAT THE CLOCK! VITE, VITE DÉPÊCHE-TOI!

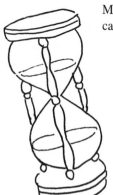

Make sure that each child has a pencil and paper. Ensure that everyone listens carefully to the instructions given in French. For example:

Ecris la date à droite en haut de la page.
Ecris ton nom à gauche en bas de la page.
Dessine une boîte au milieu de la page.
Derrière la boîte dessine un garçon.
Devant la boîte il y a une fleur.
A gauche de la boîte dessine un chien.
A droite dessine un crayon.
Entre le crayon et la boîte dessine une gomme, etc

All these instructions should be carried out as quickly as possible, so a stop-watch is a useful prop to make the game more exciting.

THE GAME OF PICASSO

This game is adapted from the children's party game *Pin the tail on the donkey* and can be rather noisy! The class is divided into teams. One child from each team is blindfolded in turn, and led to the front of the class. He or she has to draw a face on the board, with the help of the instructions shouted out by the rest of the team.

Firstly, the volunteer should draw a large circle for the face. Next, a member of the team suggests, '*Dessine les yeux*', and the other team members shout (in French), 'higher, lower, left, right', etc to guide the drawing.

The class (and the blindfolded child) repeat the pattern for the mouth, nose, ears, hair, etc, with everyone shouting out suggestions about which feature should be drawn where, each time. Whoever manages to draw the best face, as voted by the class, wins a prize or a credit.

This game allows children to gain a real understanding of prepositions and reinforces the vocabulary for describing faces, as learned previously.

L'AGENT SECRET!

Teach them how to write secret messages in code. Here is a little code and a message to decipher.

A	B	C	D	E	F	G	H	I	J	K	L	M	N	O	P	Q	R	S	T	U	V	W	X	Y	Z
Z	Y	X	W	V	U	T	S	R	Q	P	O	N	M	L	K	J	I	H	G	F	E	D	C	B	A

E.g.: JE T'AIME = QV G'ZRNV!

Ask them to send a message to one another to fix an appointment.

RENDEZ-VOUS A LA POSTE A SIX HEURES.
IVMWVA-ELFH Z OZ KLHGU Z HRC SVFIVH.

To make a code wheel: draw two circles one smaller than the other, and join them together by pushing a paper clip in the middle. Fold the legs of the paper clip back to secure the two circles together. Write the 26 letters of the alphabet around the edges of the two circles. Take special care to line up the two sets of letters. Turn the inner circle to change the code.

This is a good way of practising once more the prepositions.

AU RESTAURANT

To play this game you need to photocopy the table on the following page, one for each child, plus one for you.

Give a piece of paper to each child.

Les entrées	de la soupe de tomates	de la soupe de poulet	de la soupe de légumes
	du pâté au fromage	du saumon	du caviar
	de la salade verte	de la salade de tomates	de la salade niçoise
	du melon	du jambon	de l'avocat

Les plats du jour	de la viande	de la dinde	du poulet
	du poisson	du canard	de la viande de cheval
	du lapin	du steak	du rôti
	du saumon grillé	des boulettes	de l'omelette

Les légumes	des petits pois	des haricots	des carottes
	des pommes de terre	des aubergines	des artichauts
	des asperges	du chou-fleur	des champignons
	des frites	des oignons	du céleri

Les desserts	un gâteau à la crème	un gâteau au chocolat	un gâteau à la fraise
	une glace à la fraise	une glace à la vanille	une glace au chocolat
	une tarte aux pommes	une tarte aux fraises	une tarte aux poires
	une crème au chocolat	une salade de fruits	des fruits

Les boissons	du café	du thé	du chocolat chaud
	du coca	de l' orangina	de la limonade
	du vin blanc	du vin rouge	de la bière
	de l'eau minérale	du jus d'orange	du jus de pommes

Ask the children to draw or write three different starters in the first row: *Les Entrées*.

In the second row, three different main courses: *Les Plats du jour*

In the third row, three different vegetables: *Les Légumes*

In the fourth row, three different desserts: *Les Desserts*

In the fifth row, three different drinks: *Les Boissons*

Give each child fifteen counters; you can use some dry beans. This game is played along the same lines as *Bingo* or *Lotto*.

Cut out your own food list in sixty rectangles and put them in a bag. Pull out the rectangles one by one and call out the item of food in French, stressing *du, de la, des*. The children must cover the corresponding rectangle on the three by five grid (if they are lucky enough to have drawn it on their card!).

The first one to cover the fifteen rectangles wins. Check the winner's card and award a prize.

This is a very good way or revising the entire food vocabulary and an excellent way of learning the application of the grammatical rule governing the partitive articles: *du, de la, des*.

 ## SONGS

Songs can often be adapted to introduce new vocabulary (as with the *London Bridge* example used at the beginning of the chapter), and are easy to remember and lots of fun. In *French start* by Teresa Scibor a song is used to introduce the verb *aller* (to go). Vocabulary for particular places and the corresponding prepositions can also be introduced and repeated using this format, while practising the 'first person' part of the verb.

JE VAIS À L'ÉCOLE

Write two colour-coded lists of places to visit on the board, prefixed either by *au* or *à la,* depending on the gender of the place in question.

Using the 'going to school' version of the song below, change the words to include each of the locations on the board in turn:

in blue
au musée
au théâtre
au cinéma
au café
au club
au restaurant

in red
à la piscine
à la plage
à la banque
à la boulangerie
à l'hôtel
à l'église

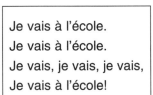

> Je vais à l'école.
> Je vais à l'école.
> Je vais, je vais, je vais,
> Je vais à l'école!

As they sing the last line, children tap their fists on the table in time with the words.

The song can be adapted as follows:

> Je vais au théâtre.
> Je vais au théâtre.
> Je vais, je vais, je vais,
> Je vais au théâtre!

Once everyone is familiar with the tune, and how to adapt the song to different places, encourage each child in turn to make up their own version of the song. Even real beginners can make up a new song using this simple format, and everyone will enjoy hearing the class sing their song.

In the excellent cassette by Vincent Heuzé *Le français en chantant,* a collection of very clever songs are used similarly to promote language learning, since they offer the chance to practise vocabulary and expression and to illustrate points of grammar in a way which may be easily remembered and which disguises the repetitive nature of much traditional grammar practice. The following example is particularly effective as a means of practising the use of prepositions through constant repetition:

LES COURSES

Play the tape, and encourage everyone to sing along and to remember the order of the words. Once the class is familiar with the original version, they can modify it according to their own suggestions and preferences.

A more advanced class can adapt the song in a more difficult exercise, combining things to buy, and shops in which to buy them, in a different verse to the same tune. Write a list of shops on the board. Also write up a list of things that might be bought from these shops. Encourage each child to invent a verse incorporating the new vocabulary.

> Ma petite maman me dit,
>
> Va très vite **à l'**épicerie,
>
> Ensuite cours **à la** pharmacie,
>
> Et puis **à la** boulangerie . . .
>
> Une salade, un citron,
>
> **Du** coton, **du** savon,
>
> Des baguettes, des bonbons.
>
> Fais bien attention . . .

in red	
à l'épicerie	de la viande
à la pharmacie	de la confiture
à la boucherie	de la salade
à la charcuterie	de la soupe
à la boulangerie	de la crème
à la pâtisserie	de la pizza
à la poissonnerie	de l'eau

in blue
du pain
du poulet
du fromage
du poisson
du saumon
du coton
du jambon
du gâteau
du lait
des spaghetti
des croissants
des biscuits
des bonbons

Rather than simply repeating phrases, the class must think about what they might buy and where, in order to compose their own rhymes. This therefore becomes a useful exercise to introduce new vocabulary, while also promoting agreements and the use of prepositions.

CILT

J'AI SOIF! J'AI FAIM!

Further examples can be found in *Un kilo de chansons* by Mary Glasgow. One of the songs from this collection can also be adapted, when the class is familiar with the tune and the format, to include other foods and drinks. Before the class begins to sing, write a list on the board, of a variety of types of food and drink, and make sure that everyone knows what each new word means. Prefix the vocabulary with *du, de l'* or *de la,* depending on whether it is masculine or feminine:

in blue

du pain	du café
du fromage	du thé
du poulet	du lait
du poisson	du vin
du jambon	du coca
du gâteau	de l'Orangina

des fruits
des biscuits
des bonbons
des légumes

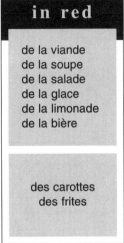

in red

de la viande
de la soupe
de la salade
de la glace
de la limonade
de la bière

des carottes
des frites

Play the tape, and encourage everyone to sing along and to remember the order of the words. Once the class is familiar with the original version, they can modify it according to their own suggestions and preferences.

Moi j'ai soif!	Moi j'ai faim!
Je voudrais un Orangina,	Je voudrais **de la** soupe.
Moi j'ai soif!	Moi, j'ai faim!
Je voudrais **du** café.	Je voudrais **du** poulet.
Tu veux **du** vin blanc?	Tu veux **du** poisson?
Non!	Non!
Tu veux **du** vin rouge?	Tu veux **du** fromage?
Non!	Non!
Tu veux **de la** bière?	Tu veux **des** bonbons?
Non, non, non!	Non, non, non!

 ## ROLE PLAY

A role play is an effective way to combine the various ideas introduced in the previous sections. Conversations and scenes can be devised to incorporate the points illustrated and to complement the new vocabulary learned. Choose a role play topic which can be easily adapted for the classroom.

A restaurant scene is perfect to introduce some simple sentences, combined with the words for food learned above. It is also very easy to set up in the classroom and, with the aid of a sheet for a tablecloth and some borrowed plates and cutlery, can look quite realistic.

While the tables are being prepared, children can write and decorate their own menus, picking a selection of food from colour-coded lists on the board. Also, write up some key phrases to help the conversation along. One child can pretend to be the waiter, while two others become the patrons, and all three children can follow the outline for the conversation about arriving in the restaurant and ordering a meal as below:

Bonjour, Monsieur/ Madame.
Bonjour.
Vous avez réservé?
Oui, une table près de la fenêtre.
Voilà. Asseyez-vous.
Merci, la carte, s'il vous plaît.
Vous désirez?
Je voudrais . . .

When asked what they would like to eat and drink, each child replies, picking three items from the list of food, and one from the selection of drinks. Having ordered, they ask for the bill and leave the restaurant:

If possible, videotape them as they are acting.

C'est tout?
Oui, l' addition s'il vous plaît.
Voilà.
Merci, au revoir.

DRING DRING!

The role play format can be adapted to include any new vocabulary that needs to be practised. Toy telephones are a useful prop for a variety of conversations, particularly for setting up meetings between people. Write the vocabulary needed on the board, and set out some key sentences to help the conversation to run smoothly. Once the class is familiar with words to describe days of the week, times and places, they can invent appointments and arrange to meet over the phone. For example:

Allô! Allô! C'est le 24 57 32 11?   *Oui.*
Bonjour Monsieur or Madame.
Monsieur...../ Madame....... est là?   *Oui, c'est moi. Qui est-ce?*
C'est ......   *Oh! Salut, ça va?*
Oui, très bien, merci.
Tu veux aller ....? (Ex: au cinéma) *Oui!*
Ex: Alors, rendez-vous le mardi
sept juin au cinéma à trois heures.

CiLT

The following lists can be written on the board, or copied down at the beginning of the class, and by practising in this way, children will quickly become familiar with the new vocabulary introduced.

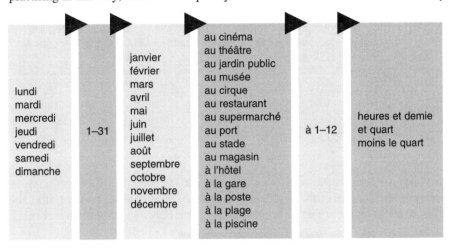

| lundi
mardi
mercredi
jeudi
vendredi
samedi
dimanche | 1–31 | janvier
février
mars
avril
mai
juin
juillet
août
septembre
octobre
novembre
décembre | au cinéma
au théâtre
au jardin public
au musée
au cirque
au restaurant
au supermarché
au port
au stade
au magasin
à l'hôtel
à la gare
à la poste
à la plage
à la piscine | à 1–12 | heures et demie
et quart
moins le quart |

The format remains the same in each example and children will become increasingly familiar with these simple sentences and the answers they require, and will hardly realise they are practising as they take on different roles. If possible, videotape them as they are acting!

LE CENTRE-VILLE

Another way to complement the vocabulary learned in the previous exercises, particularly the prepositions *au* and *à la*, and the words for different places of interest, is to involve the whole class in making a collage of a town. This exercise involves a degree of preparation beforehand.

Firstly, draw several outlines for the town buildings onto plain paper: a church, a shop, a house, a school, etc. Photocopy these outlines several times, so that each child has the outline of a building to draw and colour.

Allocate different shops to different children: the town will have a shopping centre comprising all of the following shops: *boulangerie, pâtisserie, boucherie, pharmacie, épicerie, supermarché,* together with municipal buildings such as: *banque, poste, gare, hôtel, école, garage,* etc.

Other children can also draw cars, trees, etc to make the town centre more realistic. Once all the drawings are finished and coloured in, they should be cut out carefully so that they are ready to stick on the board.

Each child should come to the front of the class in turn and stick his or her picture to the board according to the instructions you give, for example: *'Colle la boucherie à côté de l'épicerie.'*

Once all the buildings are in place on the board, the streets need to be named — either after members of staff, or children in the class! So, they become:

Boulevard du roi   *Avenue du général*
Rue de la duchesse   *Place saint*   etc.

Although preparation may be somewhat time-consuming, the exercise does provide a useful reminder of previous vocabulary, together with an introduction to the words for particular shops and buildings. Similarly, the class becomes familiar with simple commands and the vocabulary to describe the spatial relations between different objects. They also learn the words for 'colour', 'cut out' and 'stick' as they are told where to position their drawings.

Découpe	Sur
Colorie	Sous
Colle	Devant
En haut	Derrière
À gauche	À côté de
À droite	

LA COURSE AU TRÉSOR

The treasure hunt itself begins with the words, *'Il y a un trésor caché dans le centre-ville. Devinez, où est-il?'*

Beforehand, write down where the treasure is hidden, and put the piece of paper into a sealed envelope (for example, the treasure could be hidden *à la banque*). There should be a list of all the possible hiding places on the board, so that the vocabulary for all the buildings in the town is covered:

in red

à la banque
à la boucherie
à la boulangerie
à la pharmacie
à la pâtisserie
à la piscine
à la boutique

à l'épicerie
à l'école

in blue

au stade
au cinéma
au théâtre
au restaurant
au jardin
au musée
au château
au Syndicat d'Initiative
au supermarché
au magasin
au commissariat

à l'hôpital
à l'hôtel

Each child writes down three guesses of where the treasure might be hidden and puts his or her name on the piece of paper. All the guesses are then collected, and the winners announced.

THE LONGEST ADDRESS IN THE WORLD

Before the competition begins, write a long, illustrated list of prepositions on the board, as with the previous exercises: *à/aux, en, au/à la/à l', loin de, entre, à côté de, en face de, derrière, devant, sous.* Remind the class how and when to use each preposition.

The object of the competition is to try to come up with the longest address possible. Each child should imagine a place and describe where it is in relation to everything around it, so the address might read, for example: *J'habite dans une chambre dans un appartement dans un imeuble, en face de la poste, dans une rue, à côté de Belsize Park, à Hampstead, à Londres en Angleterre en Europe sur la terre . . . dans l'univers.* Award a point for each correct preposition used.

THE LONGEST SENTENCE IN THE WORLD

This is another variation of the competition to create the world's longest sentence. It is a useful way to revise all the prepositions, and much of the vocabulary introduced previously, and works on the same principle as the previous game.

Write a list of all the prepositions they have learned so far on the board, and make sure everyone remembers what each one means. Then, encourage the class to think of all the words they know in French, and write them up with their English equivalents — the board should be full of words in English and French.

Divide the class into four teams. Each team can then begin to construct, in English, the longest sentence in the world, using as many prepositions as they can to describe where things are in relation to each other. For example: There is a worm **in** an apple, **next to** a pear, **in** a basket, **behind** a vase **on** a table, **in** a kitchen, **in** a house, **in** a road, **in** Paris, etc.

Once the English sentences are as long as possible, they can be written up on the board and the whole class, with your help, can translate them into French. The example sentence above becomes:

*Il y a un ver **dans** une pomme, la pomme est **à côté de** la poire, **dans** un panier, **derrière** un vase, **sur** une table, **à la** cuisine, **dans** une maison, **dans** une rue, **à** Paris, **en** France, **en** Europe, **sur** la terre, **dans** l'univers,* etc. (You may need a dictionary to translate some of the weird and wonderful things dreamed up.)

A more advanced class can try to look up any new words themselves in a dictionary. This game is great fun and gives children the opportunity to use a variety of new prepositions. It can also highlight the differences in translation between certain prepositions — there are times when the English word 'in' can be translated in different ways, depending on the context. For example, it could be rendered as *en, à, dans, au,* etc according to the description given.

Once a more advanced class has created several sentences in this way, the competition can be adapted to team-play. Divide the children into groups of four, with one child to act as *Le chef.* Each group should devise their own Mega-sentence — they can even add colours to the description of each new object introduced, to make the sentence even longer. The winning group will have the longest accurate sentence.

CONCLUSION

Focusing on prepositions does more than simply teach children a handful of words for concepts such as 'in' or 'on'. Prepositions are an integral part of the language, and these exercises are highly effective in building up and revising new vocabulary. At the same time, the words for objects are combined with prepositions describing their relations to other objects, and so children are already beginning to construct simple sentences. Knowing whether a noun takes the preposition *au* or *à la* also reinforces the word's gender as masculine or feminine, so the language-learning process becomes one of a gradual overlapping, and reinforcing, with new concepts helping to clarify more familiar ideas. When instructions are given in French, and are accompanied by images and active participation by the class, words and phrases are easily remembered.

5.   Verbs

Without a doubt, the principal challenge that confronts any teacher of French grammar is the explanation of verbs, their conjugations, their irregularities and their application in everyday language. Nowhere are the two extremes of ineffective teaching practice more evident: ignoring conjugations and tenses on the one hand, in the hope that children will merely 'pick these things up' by some magical process; obsessive drilling on the other, as if French were a 'dead' language that existed merely to go over obscure and confusing rules.

Learning about verbs needs to be fun, but, once again, it is important not to forget that children learning a second language do not start with a clean linguistic slate, and it is pointless to pretend that they do. Many methods seem to ignore this fact, and introduce a whole lot of phrases such as *Je m'appelle . . ., J'ai sept ans, J'ai chaud, J'ai faim, J'ai soif, Il y a . . ., Il fait froid, Fais attention*, etc without giving due attention to the fact that these phrases are constructed differently to their English equivalents. **Right from the start children must be aware of similarities and differences between their language and the target language.**

Where verbs are concerned, this is particularly pertinent. It is extraordinary how many of the most common phrases we teach children early on in their learning of the language are based on a linguistic premise that is utterly confusing. For instance, the literal translation of *'Comment t'appelles-tu?'* ('What is your name?') is 'What do you call yourself?' — which children find strange initially. A good way to make them remember is to pick a child with a nickname, and illustrate how, for example, 'Tommy calls himself 'Tommy', yet his name is 'Thomas'.' The French phrase is logical, even though it might seem funny to first-time language learners. Below are other examples of ways to stress the difference between simple phrases in the two languages:

PHRASE	MEANING	LITERAL TRANSLATION
J'ai sept ans	I am seven years old	I have seven years (as if, as each year passes, they add one more)
J'ai faim	I am hungry	I have (the feeling of) hunger
J'ai froid	I am cold	I have (the feeling of) cold
J'ai sommeil	I am sleepy	I have (the feeling of) sleep
J'ai mal	It hurts/I am in pain	I have (the feeling of) pain
Il fait chaud	It is hot	It is making (a feeling of) hot
Il fait froid	It is cold	It is making (a feeling of) cold
Fais attention	Be careful	Make care
Il y a du soleil	It is sunny	It there has some sun
Il y a deux chiens	There are two dogs	It there has two dogs
Comment vas-tu?	How are you?	How do you go?
Comment ça va?	How are you?	How is it going?
Je vais bien	I am well	I go well

CiLT

All these examples illustrate how the verb 'to be' is not always translated into French as its equivalent *être*. Often, French uses different phrases to illustrate different ideas, where in English everything is rendered by 'to be'. In the French phrases above, 'to be' is often the equivalent of 'to have', 'to do', 'to go', etc.

The converse is true in the phrase: '*Zozo est arrivé*', which means 'Zozo has arrived'. In French, the phrase is 'Zozo is arrived'. In contrast to the examples above, it is the French phrase which uses 'to be' here, and in English we prefer to say 'to have'.

These are just some examples illustrating how often we run the risk of inadvertently supplying children with the wrong information about the verb 'to be'. It is hardly surprising that children who were doing brilliantly in the primary school stages are suddenly confused when faced with the conjugation of the verbs *avoir, être, aller* and *faire* at secondary school level.

What this suggests is that while we must continue to use more modern methods — games, songs, rhythm, movements, mimes and acting, with their easily learned, ready-made phrases, that hold the key to generating fluency — to their full potential, we must also insist once again that **right from the start, children must be aware of the similarities and the differences between their language and the target language**.

Each time you introduce a phrase that uses a different verb in French than the one used in English, try to promote a lively discussion about how odd it is to see the different ways in which the same idea or action can be conveyed, simply by using different images. Debate whether the class thinks that:

- 'How do you go?' is a better way of saying 'How are you?'
- 'It is making (a feeling of) cold' is a better phrase than 'It is cold'.
- 'It has there . . .' makes more sense than 'There is . . .'

Constantly remind children of these differences. Many problems can be avoided simply by reflecting logically on how someone coming across a new linguistic feature might view it. Teachers must take responsibility for **what** they teach children, as well as **how** they teach them. We must adopt a strictly disciplined approach so as not to waste children's time by teaching them unnecessary chunks of vocabulary or by giving them partial information. Our message must be clear and simple. Rules must be confronted, never ignored.

Where verbs are concerned, there are dozens of instances of small details in the usual approach to explaining a rule that is poorly thought through. For instance, take the common form *J'ai*. Many teachers have doubtless had to correct (or choose to ignore) the fact that many children put the apostrophe all over the place: before the *J*, on top of the *J*, on the *a*, etc. If we explain to children, right from the start, that *J'ai* stands for *Je ai*, and *J'habite* stands for *Je habite,* and that we have had to cross out the *e* because French people don't like the sound of the two vowels following one another, the rule is much harder to forget. Explain that it follows the same sort of pattern as the articles *le* and *l',* and is a bit like English, when we use 'an' instead of 'a' — for example, 'an apple'.

If the rule is clear from the start, when reflexive verbs are introduced, they will be understood immediately. For example, *Je m'habille.*

Similarly, when introducing the negative, many primary school books simply say, 'Just put *ne* before the verb and *pas* after the verb'. Although this statement serves its purpose in the primary stages, it is very confusing later on when children have to tackle more complex sentence construction. For example: *Il ne s'appelle pas Jean; Nous n'y allons pas souvent; Elle ne lui donne pas de crayons; Tu n'en as pas.* The *ne* is not placed immediately before the verb in these cases, and confusion easily arises. A more correct statement would be: Place the *ne* straight after the subject and the *pas* straight after the verb!

Such details have to be dealt with as early as possible. Ignoring them simply means that one cannot give children a full range of possibilities within which to explore verbs as they learn them. Taking this into consideration, the key to the method is, once more, the gradual use of different games to build confidence and accuracy.

What follows is a selection of classroom games to help children to familiarise themselves with the rather complex way different verbs are conjugated.

INTRODUCING *TU* AND *VOUS*

This exercise builds up awareness of the difference between the second person singular and the second person plural with a game of *Simon dit . . .*

In this method, the game *Simon says . . .* is often employed in different contexts to get children talking and listening and can easily be adapted by taking the game one step further.

One child stands up. When you give your order for example: *'Jacques dit regarde à gauche'* the child standing has to respond, but if you say: *'Jacques dit regardez à gauche'*, the whole class must follow the command. The format is almost the same as before, but one small change makes all the difference. A whole understanding of the difference in the conjugation of the second person singular and the second person plural is immediately gained.

INTRODUCING *-ER* VERBS: *LES VERBES DU PREMIER GROUPE*

Write a list of first group verbs (those ending in *-er*) on the board. Make sure that the class understands the format and the meanings of the verbs in front of them:

sauter	chanter	danser	regarder	marcher	écouter
je saute tu sautes	je chante tu chantes	je danse tu danses	je regarde tu regardes	je marche tu marches	j'écoute tu écoutes

dessiner	entrer	tomber	manger	fermer	allumer
je dessine tu dessines	j'entre tu entres	je tombe tu tombes	je mange tu manges	je ferme tu fermes	j'allume tu allumes

CiLT

Les verbes en -er

nager

briller

marcher

voyager

grimper

pleurer

regarder

patiner

aboyer

chauffer

écouter

sécher

caresser

donner

aimer

glisser

tomber

entrer

Point out that the *tu* ending of the verb has a silent *s*. Also, explain that *J'écoute* stands for *Je écoute*, as in the previous *j'* example.

Again, the differences introduced can best be explained through a miming game. Here, each child in turn mimes a verb. The class guesses what is being mimed, saying for example: '*Tu sautes?*' to which the child replies, '*Oui, je saute*'.

Take the game one step further by using verbs in the plural form.

Write a similar table on the board and explain the format, as above:

sauter	chanter	danser	regarder	marcher	écouter
nous sautons vous sautez	nous chantons vous chantez	nous dansons vous dansez	nous regardons vous regardez	nous marchons vous marchez	nous écoutons vous écoutez

dessiner	entrer	tomber	manger	fermer	allumer
nous dessinons vous dessinez	nous entrons vous entrez	nous tombons vous tombez	nous mangeons vous mangez	nous fermons vous fermez	nous allumons vous allumez

Ask a group of children to mime one of the verbs from the list. The class has to guess which one is being mimed, by saying for example: '*Vous dansez?*' If they guess correctly, the group answers '*Oui, nous dansons.*'

LES CROIX ET LES RONDS: STARTING WITH ACHETER

The overhead projector can facilitate the task of teaching verbs. For instance, by starting with a very simple grid (three by three on a transparency), we can play a game of noughts and crosses to practise some verb endings.

If you cannot get hold of an overhead projector, you can still play the game by sticking nine pictures on the board with Blu-tack. Use 'Post-it' notes to mark the 'x's and the 'o's.

Divide the class into four teams. Each member of the first team (*les croix*) plays, in turn, against each member of the second team (*les ronds*). The two other teams then play against each other in the same way.

At the end of the matches, the winning teams play in the final. To put a *croix* or a *rond* on a square, children have to create a phrase correctly, without conferring or prompting, by following the instructions you give. The first team that manages to get three noughts or three crosses in a row, in any direction, wins the game.

Acheter is a member of the 'first group' of verbs. With some slight modifications, it behaves regularly. Once these modifications have been explained (i.e. there is no accent in the first and second person plural forms), the verb can be used as a handy example.

Once everyone knows the conjugation of the verb, write the different personal pronouns in the noughts and crosses grid on the board, one pronoun for each square on the grid. (You could also write the conjugation of the verb at the side of the board to help them initially.)

Each team (*l'équipe*) should then indicate where they want you to place their *croix* or *rond* by saying the pronoun in that box. The teams should then match the correct part of the verb with the pronoun they have chosen. If they think there is an accent on that part of the verb, they must salute with their right hand to show which way the accent slants.

J'achète
Tu achètes
Il achète
Elle achète
On achète
Nous achetons
Vous achetez
Ils achètent
Elles achètent

CILT

J'	Elle	Vous
Tu	On	Ils
Il	Nous	Elles

Making the game more complicated, and introducing actions, adds to the fun.

Depending on the level of the class, you can prepare different overlays to help to construct simple sentences. Make another overlay as before. In each square write a different type of shop. So, for a square with the word *boulangerie,* in which the pronoun *Je* is also written, the sentence should be *J'achète du pain à la boulangerie.* **Initially it may help to have a list of vocabulary written up at the side, just until the class becomes more familiar with how the sentences are constructed.** A class might be expected to create sentences, such as: *Elle achète de la viande à la boucherie* or *Vous achetez une robe à la boutique.*

This game can easily be adapted to introduce a variety of new vocabulary and ideas.

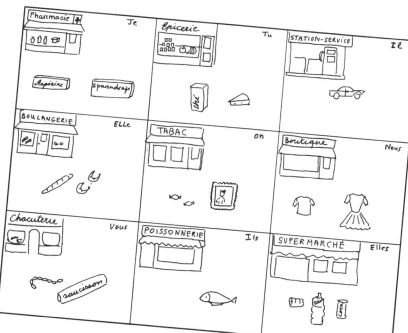

in blue

du poulet
du lait
du pain
du jambon
du sparadrap
du raisin
un T-shirt
un chapeau
un timbre

in red

de la confiture
de la viande
de l'eau minérale
des pommes
des oranges
des antibiotiques
une robe
une veste
des chaussures

LES ANIMAUX

The use of several common verb forms and the game of noughts and crosses can be combined to revise a range of different verb endings. Using the same grid as before, draw a different animal on each square. Colour-code some helpful phrases on an overlay, or write a list at the side of the board, separating masculine and feminine genders as before.

Again, to choose a particular square, the team must name the animal drawn in it, saying for example: '*C'est un lapin*'. Only then can they claim that square as a *croix* or a *rond*.

Once the rabbit has been chosen, they can invent a name for it, such as: *Il s'appelle Bunny*. Ask the class how old they think it might be. They might reply, for example: '*Il a un an*'; and finally, get them to choose an adjective to describe Bunny: '*Il est mignon*'.

in blue

Il s'appelle
Il a . . . an(s)
Il est . . .
grand
beau
méchant
adorable
petit
mignon

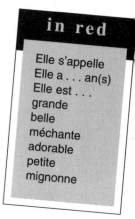

in red

Elle s'appelle
Elle a . . . an(s)
Elle est . . .
grande
belle
méchante
adorable
petite
mignonne

Again, schematic prompts such as these train children to express themselves with ease, and eventually to write correctly. It is much less daunting for them to construct sentences when all the constituent elements are in front of them, so care can be given instead to pronunciation and agreements, and the exercise becomes entertaining.

The same format could equally be used to talk about people. Draw a different character in each square of the grid. For a more advanced class, the game might involve children providing a description of the person and what they are wearing.

 ## INTRODUCING THE VERB *ALLER*

Prepare a grid as before with a different pronoun in each square. Draw a selection of the places you would like them to practise on an overlay. On another overlay conjugate the verb *aller* on the left hand side, and on the other side write down the names of the places pictured in columns, depending on whether they are masculine or feminine (prefixed, *au* or *à la*).

Je vais Tu vas Il va Elle va On va Nous allons Vous allez Ils vont

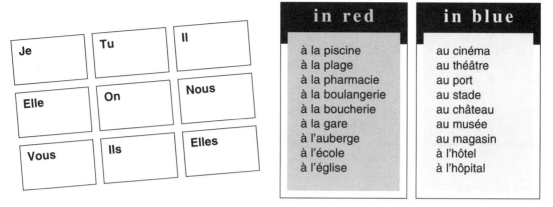

Je	Tu	Il
Elle	On	Nous
Vous	Ils	Elles

in red	in blue
à la piscine	au cinéma
à la plage	au théâtre
à la pharmacie	au port
à la boulangerie	au stade
à la boucherie	au château
à la gare	au musée
à l'auberge	au magasin
à l'école	à l'hôtel
à l'église	à l'hôpital

Initially, practise the different parts of the verb by highlighting different pronouns with noughts or crosses as before. When a team chooses a pronoun, they should say the corresponding part of the verb *aller* to be awarded a nought or a cross. After a few attempts at the exercise, they should also add the word for the place that is drawn on that square, remembering to use the correct preposition.

In this way children can familiarise themselves with the present tense of the verb *aller*. Ensure that each part of the verb is properly pronounced, and remind them that *nous* and *vous* have a silent *s* at the end. However, when these pronouns are followed by a word starting with a vowel, the pronunciation changes to a *z* sound, as before, and becomes: *Nou . . . zallons, Vou . . . zallez*.

A more advanced group could add when they are going to that particular place by naming the day of the week : *le lundi, le mardi, le mercredi, le jeudi, le vendredi, le samedi, le dimanche*.

JOUER AU OR FAIRE DU?

LES SPORTS

Use a game of noughts and crosses to illustrate the difference between *jouer au . . .* and *faire du . . .*

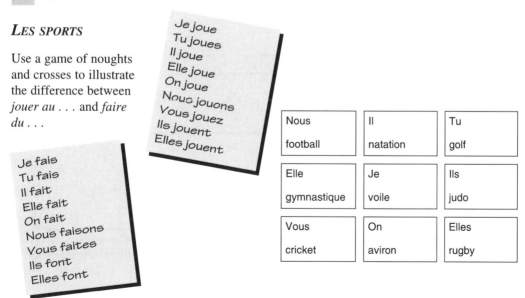

Je joue
Tu joues
Il joue
Elle joue
On joue
Nous jouons
Vous jouez
Ils jouent
Elles jouent

Je fais
Tu fais
Il fait
Elle fait
On fait
Nous faisons
Vous faites
Ils font
Elles font

Nous football	Il natation	Tu golf
Elle gymnastique	Je voile	Ils judo
Vous cricket	On aviron	Elles rugby

Sports that are spelt the same in French and English are masculine.

For all ball games that are masculine use:

Jouer au . . .

football cricket base-ball basket rugby

Some sports are masculine but are not ball games. For these use:

Faire du . . .

ski judo surf patinage karaté

Some sports are feminine and are not ball games. For these use:

Faire de la . . .

natation boxe lutte gymnastique voile

Some sports start with a vowel and are not ball games. For these use:

Faire de l' . . .

escrime escalade aviron équitation

A more advanced group could add when they practise this particular sport: *en été, en automne, en hiver, au printemps.*

C**i**LT

Introducing *Être*

Chanting

Regine Llorca, in *Les rythmimots,* introduces the verb *être* via a chanting exercise (similar to the idea of using tunes and rhythm to illustrate new grammatical ideas explored in previous examples) with some added rhythmic steps.

> Je suis
> Tu es
> Il est
> Elle est
> On est
> Nous sommes
> Vous êtes
> Ils sont
> Elles sont

For this exercise, four volunteers are needed, two boys and two girls. Give each volunteer a French name of one syllable, for example: Marc, Brice, Anne and Lise. Ask them to come to the front of the class and stand in line — boy, girl, boy, girl — facing the others.

The rest of the class acts as the orchestra and accompanies them by clapping their hands or clicking their fingers. Marc, Brice, Anne and Lise must chant each syllable in time with a step forwards or backwards.

First sequence:

'***Je** suis **Marc**'.* — The first child steps forward. As he says the word '*Je*', he stamps his right foot. As he says '*Marc*', he stamps his left foot and stops.

'***Je** suis **Brice**'.* — Brice repeats this format: as he says the word '*Je*', he stamps his right foot, and he stamps his left as he says '*Brice*', and stops.

'***Nous** sommes **frères**'.* — Marc and Brice step backwards together. As they say '*Nous*', they step back with their left foot. As they say '*frères*', they step back with their right, and then stop.

The two girls then follow, chanting and stamping as before. '***Je** suis **Anne**'. '**Je** suis **Lise**'*, marking the '*je*' and the '*Anne*' or '*Lise*' with a step forward. When they chant '***Nous** sommes **sœurs**',* they both step backwards, in time.

'***Je** suis **Marc**', '**Je** suis **Anne**', '**Je** suis **Brice**', **Je** suis **Lise**'.* The four children take a step forward in turn, and chant again to mark each syllable. Finally they chant '***Nous** sommes **frères** et **sœurs**',* taking two steps back together. (They put one foot down on '*nous*', the other on '*frères*', they then mark the last movement for the syllable '*sœurs*' by crossing their arms.)

These two sequences allow the class to experiment with different pronouns and different forms of the verb *être*.

Second sequence:

The four volunteers continue to pace in time, while the rest of the class introduces them as they step forwards and backwards as before:

> '***Voici Marc**, **voici Brice**, **ils** sont **frères**.*
> ***Voici Anne**, **voici Lise**, **elles** sont **sœurs***
> ***Voici Marc**, **voici Anne**, **voici Brice**, **voici Lise**,*
> ***ils** sont **frères** et **sœurs**'.*

Third sequence:

One child (or several children) from the rest of the class addresses Marc and Brice, Anne and Lise directly, saying:

'*Tu es Marc, tu es Brice, vous êtes frères*
Tu es Anne, tu es Lise, vous êtes sœurs
Tu es Marc, tu es Anne, tu es Brice, tu es Lise, vous êtes frères et sœurs.'

By varying the exercise in this way, each part of the verb can be practised. There are many possible variations of this exercise. Children could be asked to improvise and build their own sentences, for example. They don't necessarily have to use the verb *être,* but they have to respect the tempo, and mark it by rythmic steps in the same way.

MIME

In Chapter 2 a mime game was introduced to explain the use of adjectives and their agreements. Once the class is familiar with the game, and with the emotions mimed, the same format can be taken one step further to include descriptions of how several people feel at once. This introduces the differences between *Ils* and *Elles* and shows how adjectives also agree in the plural. It is important to explain that *Il* and *Elle,* like 'He' and 'She' become 'They' when referring to more than one person.

Write on the board:

```
nous sommes . . . vous êtes . . . ils sont . . . elles sont . . .
```

Prepare little cards as illustrated on p17. Divide the class into small teams. Ask one child to choose a card for his or her team to mime. This time, the class has to guess what they are miming, using the plural form. For example: '*Ils sont heureux*', or '*Elles sont heureuses*'.

This game can be further supplemented with a class discussion about the fact that even if thirty girls and only one boy did the miming, we have to refer to them as '*Ils*' and not '*Elles*'.

In a further development, several children can be grouped together to mime a particular job. The rest of the class guesses their profession, but substitutes the phrase '*Vous êtes . . .*' for the phrase '*Tu es . . .*' in the first example. Similarly, the group miming answers: '*Oui, nous sommes . . .*' when the class guesses correctly.

Not only are they aware of agreements according to gender, but the idea of a plural form can now be introduced. Over the course of these miming games, the class becomes familiar with new agreements of nouns, verbs and adjectives, and it is important to check that the pronunciation is correct, and that these new concepts are properly understood.

These exercises practise the personal pronouns *nous, vous, ils, elles*. It should be stressed that their usual pronunciation is without sounding the *s*. However, since the verb *être* is one early example of a verb which causes this pronunciation to alter, it is helpful to introduce this change by getting the class to think of the *s* bouncing onto the verb *être* and becoming a *z*! So to obtain the correct pronunciation of the phrase *vous êtes,* the change is illustrated as *vou zêtes.*

'DRILLING' THE CONJUGATION OF ÊTRE

The verb *être* can also be illustrated with another familiar children's game. Make sure everyone has a square piece of paper. Fold it in half lengthways, and open it up again leaving a crease. Fold in half widthways in the same way (see Fig a).

Fold the corners in half towards the middle point and press down (see Figs b and c).

Turn it over (see Fig d).

Fold the corners towards the middle point again (see Figs e and f).

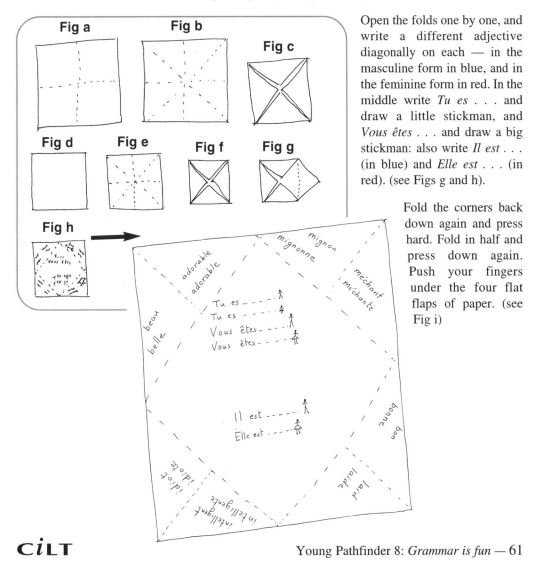

Open the folds one by one, and write a different adjective diagonally on each — in the masculine form in blue, and in the feminine form in red. In the middle write *Tu es . . .* and draw a little stickman, and *Vous êtes . . .* and draw a big stickman: also write *Il est . . .* (in blue) and *Elle est . . .* (in red). (see Figs g and h).

Fold the corners back down again and press hard. Fold in half and press down again. Push your fingers under the four flat flaps of paper. (see Fig i)

This opens the folded shape into a kind of pyramid. Once everyone has both thumbs and forefingers under the flaps, they can open and shut the shape, like a beak.

Fig i

After this preparation, the game can be played in pairs, with one child moving the paper, and the other choosing a phrase from the corners that are visible each time. As the paper is moved open and shut, different options are revealed.

INTRODUCING *AVOIR*

LA BATAILLE NAVALE

The game of *Battleships* can easily be adapted to practise verbs and simple sentences. On a piece of A4 paper draw two grids with ten columns and eight rows in each. Beginning in the second column, write above each subsequent column one of the following pronouns: *je, tu, il, elle, on, nous, vous, ils* and *elles,* and the corresponding form of the verb *avoir* in the present tense.

Along the first column, again starting from the second row, write or draw the name of a different animal. Perpare one photocopy per child before beginning the exercise. The two grids should be identical, and should look like the example below:

	J'ai	Tu as	Il a	Elle a	On a	Nous avons	Vous avez	Ils ont	Elles ont
un chat									
un chien									
une souris									
un cheval									
un canard									
un hamster									
un serpent									
une tortue									

Divide the class into pairs. Both players should secretly place six crosses anywhere on the first grid. There should never be two adjacent crosses on any grid. Each player calls out one shot on his turn aimed at one position on the opponent's grid. His or her guess should comprise the pronoun and verb followed by an animal.

When fired upon, each player must immediately say if the shot has hit or missed one of the crosses on his or her grid. If it has missed, the child guessing marks the square with *un rond,* if it has hit, he or she marks the square with *une croix* and surrounds it with *des ronds* on all sides. The object of the game is to locate all six crosses on the opponent's grid.

CiLT

Below are further examples of *Bataille navale*. The first one illustrates the differences between French and English. Here, if a part of the body hurts, in French we say 'I have (the feeling of) pain'.

	J'ai mal	Tu as mal	Il a mal	Elle a mal	On a mal	Nous avons mal	Vous avez mal	Ils ont mal	Elles ont mal
à la tête									
au pied									
aux oreilles									
au ventre									
au doigt									
aux yeux									
au dos									

	J'ai	Tu as	Il a	Elle a	On a	Nous avons	Vous avez	Ils ont	Elles ont
un an									
froid									
chaud									
peur									
sommeil									
soif									
faim									
honte									

The same principle can be adapted further to practise the present tense of other verbs, such as *aller,* and also the prepositions *au, à la, à l'* and *aux* as introduced previously, to ensure that everyone understands the distinctions between these forms.

	Je vais	Tu vas	Il va	Elle va	On va	Nous allons	Vous allez	Ils vont	Elles vont
à la plage									
aux magasins									
au port									
à l'hôtel									
au commissariat									
à la boulangerie									
à l'épicerie									

	J'achète	Tu achètes	Il achète	Elle achète	On achète	Nous achetons	Vous achetez	Ils achètent	Elles achètent
de la viande									
du poisson									
des carottes									
du poulet									
de l'eau									
du sucre									
du vin									

	Je porte	Tu portes	Il porte	Elle porte	On porte	Nous portons	Vous portez	Ils portent	Elles portent
des chaussures									
une chemise									
un pantalon									
une robe									
une veste									
un anorak									
une cravate									

These games are fun, but also illustrate important nuances of verb and sentence construction, involving constant practice and concentration.

BEAT THE CLOCK

Ask everyone in the class to draw their family as best they can and label each one *mon père, ma mère,* and so on, according to the people they represent. The children should also write down three sentences relating to three members of their family pictured.

Each child in turn has half a minute to read out his or her sentences introducing the three members of his or her family to the rest of the class. Again, the exercise can be made more exciting by timing each child with a stopwatch or egg-timer. You could even tape their descriptions and play them back to the class.

Write a few phrases on the board, making sure that everyone understands the format:

Voici mon père.	Il s'appelle . . .	Il a . . . ans.	Il porte . . .	Il est . . .
Voici mon frère.	Il s'appelle . . .	Il a . . . ans.	Il porte . . .	Il est . . .
Voici ma mère.	Elle s'appelle . . .	Elle a . . . ans.	Elle porte . . .	Elle est . . .
Voici ma sœur.	Elle s'appelle . . .	Elle a . . . ans.	Elle porte . . .	Elle est . . .

It is always important to provide schematic prompts to train children to write sentences down correctly, and to express themselves with ease.

You could also have a special day where children can bring their favourite soft toy into school and introduce it to the class. Write a few key phrases on the board. Explain the format to stress the pattern the introductions should follow:

in blue	**in red**
Il s'appelle	Elle s'appelle
Il a . . . ans	Elle a . . . ans
Il est beau	Elle est belle
. . . grand	. . . grande
. . . petit	. . . petite
. . . mignon	. . . mignonne
. . . adorable	. . . adorable
. . . méchant	. . . méchante
Il porte . . .	Elle porte . . .

INTRODUCING THE NEGATIVE

'NE RIS PAS!'

A little elimination game similar to the familiar party game *Dead lions.*
Before you start the game, write on the board :

Explain what every phrase means. Draw their attention to *ne* and *pas.*

Ask all the children to lie down on the floor or put their head on the
desk and pretend to be dead. '*Vous êtes morts!*'

> Ne bouge pas
>
> Ne ris pas
>
> Ne parle pas
>
> Ne baille pas
>
> Ne souris pas
>
> Ne respire pas

Once the game starts, they are not
allowed to move. Walk round the
classroom saying: '*Ne bouge
pas! Ne ris pas! Ne parle pas! Ne respire pas!*'
Change the intonation of your voice. The one who is caught
giggling, talking or moving is out.

This is a settling game and a good introduction to the negative.

THE REFLEXIVE VERBS

Introduce the reflexive verbs with a song from the
cassette *French start* by Teresa Scibor.

'VITE! VITE! DÉPÊCHE-TOI!'

For this game you need some blank cards
(54 cards per set). Prepare four sets of cards like
the one below. Mark each set with a different symbol.

> Je me lève.
> Je me lave.
> Je me brosse les dents.
> Je m'habille.
> Je mange un petit croissant.
> Je sors.
> Je dis Au revoir Maman.
> Au revoir Maman.

Je	Tu	Il	Elle	On	Nous	Vous	Ils	Elles
Je	Tu	Il	Elle	On	Nous	Vous	Ils	Elles
Je	Tu	Il	Elle	On	Nous	Vous	Ils	Elles
joue	joues	joue	joue	joue	jouons	jouez	jouent	jouent
suis	es	est	est	est	sommes	êtes	sont	sont
ai	as	a	a	a	avons	avez	ont	ont

Divide the class in four teams. Set up an alarm clock or a timer. Give a set of cards to each team. They have twelve minutes to pair the cards and form the correct conjugation of the verbs *avoir, être* and *jouer*.

For a more advanced group you could add one more verb: *Faire*.

Je	Tu	Il	Elle	On	Nous	Vous	Ils	Elles
fais	fais	fait	fait	fait	faisons	faites	font	font

CONCLUSION

By continually providing children with oral examples, checklists, colour-coded mnemonics and grids, you encourage them to express themselves correctly. By experimenting and using the language with the aid of schematic prompts, they can assimilate subconsciously the concept of the first, second and third person singular and plural forms, and build a solid foundation for understanding the mechanisms of verbs. They feel secure and learn without effort. Train their minds to see the beautiful patterns the French language makes. A whole universe of verbs and conjugation can be opened up both naturally and engagingly. The result, in my experience, can be staggering.

ciLT

6. Introducing adverbs

When introducing a new grammar concept, it is often useful to illustrate the idea, and its application, with games or songs which are already familiar to the class — either adapting games used to clarify previous points, or, as with the example below, using a well-known French rhyme and adapting it to explain a particular grammatical point.

Once the class is familiar with how to use verbs, and their different forms in the present tense, the use of adverbs to qualify actions can also be illustrated. The example below adapts the rhyme 'She loves me, she loves me not', usually chanted as petals are pulled from a daisy. The verb used will be *aimer* each time, but the adverb will vary to describe the extent to which 'she loves me'.

SHE LOVES ME

The game is very easy to prepare. Either take the class outside to each find a daisy, or collect enough flowers beforehand for each member of the class to have one. Explain that, for the boys, the rhyme will be *Elle m'aime,* and for the girls, *Il m'aime,* and that, in French, it is not whether she or he loves me or not that counts, but **how much** I am loved.

Prepare a list of the relevant adverbs beforehand and, as they pull off each petal one by one, tell the class to work their way down the list of adverbs on the board. So, the rhyme becomes:

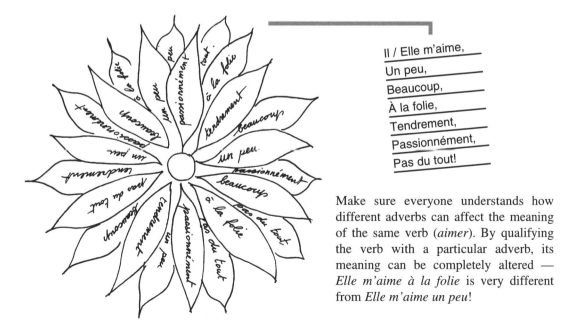

Il / Elle m'aime,
Un peu,
Beaucoup,
À la folie,
Tendrement,
Passionnément,
Pas du tout!

Make sure everyone understands how different adverbs can affect the meaning of the same verb (*aimer*). By qualifying the verb with a particular adverb, its meaning can be completely altered — *Elle m'aime à la folie* is very different from *Elle m'aime un peu*!

L'ESCLAVE

Once the concept of adverbs has been introduced and illustrated using one verb, use a game of *L'esclave de la classe!* to show how the same principles can apply to all verbs. Pick a selection of verbs and write them, in the infinitive, on the board. Encourage the class to read each verb out loud, and ensure that everyone understands what each word means. The following selection of verbs might be used and adapted:

regarder	ouvrir	fermer	manger	parler	chanter	crier
marcher	sauter	danser	lever	baisser	inspecter	chercher
dessiner	colorier	cocher	arrêter	ranger	ramasser	mettre
apporter	ecrire	avancer	aller	venir	reculer	aligner
effacer	allumer	pousser				

Repeat, with a list of adverbs such as:

Check pronunciation and meaning again.

vite	doucement
lentement	gentiment
mal	distraitement
bien	difficilement
brusquement	

Give the class a few minutes to think about how each adverb will affect the verbs in the list, altering their meaning.

The game itself consists of one child miming a verb chosen by the class from the first list, in the style of a particular adverb from the second list, so it is important to ensure that both verbs and adverbs are clear to everyone before beginning.

Before playing, write each adverb onto a small card and put all the cards into a box at the front of the class. Pick one child to mime first. He or she selects an adverb card from the box and is careful not to show it to anyone else. When the class has chosen a verb from the list, the child acts out that verb in the style of the adverb on the card.

For example, if the class picks the verb *marcher* (to walk), their command will be '*Marche*'. If the adverb on the card is *vite,* the child must walk quickly, so that the class can guess the adverb picked.

To make a suggestion, the class should combine verb and adverb in a simple sentence, so their guess becomes: '*Tu marches vite?*', to which the child miming replies: '*Oui, je marche vite*'.

These simple sentences allow children to practise the first and second person singular forms of each verb (*je/tu*), and highlight how the use of adverbs enhances the description of what someone is doing. Once the class understands how, and when, to use adverbs and different parts of the verb, the game can be adapted so that several children mime at once.

This is an easy way to introduce the *nous* and *vous* forms of each verb, to show how verbs can apply to more than one person, and how they must change to do so. Make sure they know how to make the *nous* and *vous* forms of the verb, and adapt the questions accordingly:

CiLT

The guess becomes: '*Vous marchez vite?*' to which those miming reply: '*Oui, nous marchons vite*', etc.

At the same time, introduce the idea that *tu* and *vous* can both be used for one person — they might say *tu* to refer to their friends, but if they talk to a teacher, or another adult, they should always use the *vous* form out of politeness.

Once the class understands the difference between the *tu* and *vous* forms, and when to use them, you can volunteer to be *l'esclave,* and to obey their every command, **provided that they always refer to you as *vous* when guessing and commanding.**

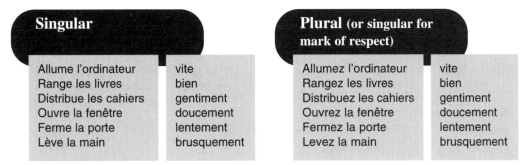

Singular		**Plural** (or singular for mark of respect)	
Allume l'ordinateur	vite	Allumez l'ordinateur	vite
Range les livres	bien	Rangez les livres	bien
Distribue les cahiers	gentiment	Distribuez les cahiers	gentiment
Ouvre la fenêtre	doucement	Ouvrez la fenêtre	doucement
Ferme la porte	lentement	Fermez la porte	lentement
Lève la main	brusquement	Levez la main	brusquement

NI OUI, NI NON

Write a selection of possible answers from this list on the board:

Jamais	Toujours	Quelquefois
Rarement	Souvent	De temps en temps
Pas du tout	Parfois	Peut-être
Ce n'est pas vrai	Certainement	C'est un secret!
C'est impossible	Evidemment	
Je doute	Normalement	
Je ne crois pas	Naturellement	
	C'est possible	
	C'est vrai	

Go over all the different expressions explaining what each one means. Ask the children to read them and make sure they pronounce them correctly. Point out all the adverbs to them.

Then ask them to answer your questions in French without using *Oui* or *Non*. At first they can make use of the list of adverbs provided to answer and take their time to answer, but as they gain confidence, play the game faster and faster.

Some examples of questions:

Tu t'appelles Jean?
Tu vas à l'école?
Tu aimes l'école?
Ton chat va à l'école?
Ton école s'appelle Marks and Spencer?
Tu joues au football le lundi?
Ta grand-mère joue au football?
Tu as un frère?

Ton frère est petit?
Il s'appelle Marc?
Tu habites une maison?
Ta maison a vingt chambres?
Tu aimes les tarentules?
Tu aimes Liliane?
Liliane est belle?

LE JEU DE CONSÉQUENCES

Write on the board:

(Le nom d'un homme ou d'un garçon)
a rencontré
(Le nom d'une fille ou d'une femme)
à la ...... au .... à l' ....
Elle lui a dit ....
(Adverbe)
Il lui a dit ....
(Adverbe)
(Conséquence ....)

Make a list of some adverbs they can use:

gentiment
doucement
amoureusement
timidement
passionnément
calmement
majestueusement
vite
brusquement
soudainement
cruellement
méchamment
stupidement
bêtement

- Give a thin strip of paper to each child. Ask them to start the game by writing the name of a man or boy at the top of the paper.
- The paper is then folded over and passed to the next child who has to add: *a rencontré*, followed by a lady's or a girl's name.
- The paper is again folded and passed on. They then have to write in French where they met (using *au, à la à l'*).
- The paper is folded and they have to write. '*Elle lui a dit*' + an adverb. Paper is folded and passed on. They have to write what she said.
- The paper is folded and then passed on. They have to write: *Il lui a dit* + an adverb. The paper is folded and passed on. They have to write what he said.
- The paper is folded and passed on. They have to write the consequence. The papers are unfolded and read out aloud.

This little game is very popular with ten- to twelve-year old children. Encourage them to speak in French: *C'est mon tour. C'est ton tour. Écris. Vite. Plie le papier. Passe le papier. Lis.*

Qu'est-ce que tu fais pour aider à la maison **?**

(Coche la bonne case)

	Toujours	Souvent	Parfois	Jamais
Je mets la table	☐	☐	☐	☐
Je mets de l'ordre	☐	☐	☐	☐
Je lave la vaisselle	☐	☐	☐	☐
Je lave la voiture	☐	☐	☐	☐
Je passe l'aspirateur	☐	☐	☐	☐
Je repasse	☐	☐	☐	☐
Je promène le chien	☐	☐	☐	☐

Qu'est-ce que tu fais le week-end **?**

(Coche la bonne case)

	Toujours	Souvent	Parfois	Jamais
Je vais au cinéma	☐	☐	☐	☐
Je vais au restaurant	☐	☐	☐	☐
Je joue au foot	☐	☐	☐	☐
Je fais de la gymnastique	☐	☐	☐	☐
Je fais mes devoirs	☐	☐	☐	☐
Je regarde la télévision	☐	☐	☐	☐
Je reste à la maison	☐	☐	☐	☐

Qu'est-ce que tu aimes **?**

(Coche la bonne case)

	Beaucoup	Un peu	Pas vraiment	Pas du tout
Tu aimes l'école?	☐	☐	☐	☐
Tu aimes les animaux?	☐	☐	☐	☐
Tu aimes le cinéma?	☐	☐	☐	☐
Tu aimes la musique jazz?	☐	☐	☐	☐
Tu aimes les sports?	☐	☐	☐	☐

The previous exercises have illustrated the ways in which adverbs qualify verbs, and have introduced and revised the forms of the verbs themselves. However, they do not explain how adverbs are constructed — how an adjective can be altered to become an adverb.

One exercise to illustrate this notion is the competition, *Beat the clock!*, which comprises lists of adjectives and their corresponding adverbs, to show how the latter are constructed.

LA COURSE À LA MONTRE! (BEAT THE CLOCK!)

Prepare for the competition by drawing up a selection from this list of adjectives — in colour-coded columns for the masculine and feminine forms once more — on the board. Also write down a list of the corresponding adverbs, **though not in the same order as the lists of adjectives**. It is important to distinguish between the masculine and feminine forms of the adjectives, to illustrate more clearly how the feminine form is adapted to form the adverb.

certain	certaine	certainement
naturel	naturelle	naturellement
furieux	furieuse	furieusement
merveilleux	merveilleuse	merveilleusement
majestueux	majestueuse	majestueusement
extraordinaire	extraordinaire	extraordinairement
soudain	soudaine	soudainement
fantastique	fantastique	fantastiquement
adorable	adorable	adorablement
agressif	agressive	agressivement
agilement	agile	agilement
large	large	largement
long	longue	longuement
systématique	systématique	systématiquement
complet	complète	complètement
actuel	actuelle	actuellement
officiel	officielle	officiellement
habituel	habituelle	habituellement
général	générale	généralement
généreux	généreuse	généreusement
dangereux	dangereuse	dangereusement
stupide	stupide	stupidement
tendre	tendre	tendrement
timide	timide	timidement
horrible	horrible	horriblement
difficile	difficile	difficilement
dangereux	dangereuse	dangereusement
vrai	vraie	vraiment
absolu	absolue	absolument

For example:

soudain	dangereuse	soudainement
majestueux	horrible	dangereusement
tendre	soudaine	tendrement
horrible	lente	timidement
stupide	tendre	majestueusement
absolu	adorable	horriblement
dangereux	stupide	absolument
adorable	timide	stupidement
lent	absolue	adorablement
timide	majestueuse	lentement

Bring in an egg timer, or a stopwatch, and give the class three minutes to match up the adjectives with their corresponding adverbs. The winners of the competition are those who manage to match all the adverbs to their adjectives correctly.

Once the adjectives and adverbs have been matched up, the class should practise the pronunciation of the words, and establish what each one means. Many of the words chosen here are recognisable from their English equivalents; this is reassuring when introducing a new concept, since the two languages can often appear to be very different, and the experience of the foreign language rather alienating. Instead of explaining the meaning of each adverb/adjective, encourage the class to establish for themselves what each might signify, and how the adverb might be formed in each case.

7. Asking questions

The ability to formulate questions accurately and fluently is an essential component of mastering a language. **Right from the start children should be encouraged to ask questions in French.** Because asking questions in French involves the use of some words which are difficult to read or pronounce, it is helpful to use rhythm and music as well as games to facilitate the task. Language associated with music — a rap or a jingle — can be used to practise complicated pronunciation and can provide the means to experiment with, and master, new sounds which are often more easily remembered in this context.

SONGS

Any well-known tune or rhyme can be adapted, with a little imagination, to illustrate a particular point, as we have seen in previous chapters. The only criteria are that the verse should have lots of repetition — with easy, short phrases — and the tune should be lively and 'catchy'. *Le français par le chant* by Dominique Field and Alex Forbes is a very useful cassette, comprising lots of songs which illustrate a variety of grammatical nuances. One particular example on the tape is '*Bonjour*', which introduces the means to ask simple questions.

> Bonjour
> Bonjour,
> Bonjour.
> Comment t'appelles tu?
> Je m'appelle . . .
> Je m'appelle . . .
> Et toi?
> Et toi?
> Bonjour.

As in Chapter 4, remind the class that French sometimes uses different phrases to express the same English idea. Instead of 'My name is . . .' the French prefer to say, 'I call myself . . .' In Chapter 4 this was illustrated by picking a child with a nickname (my example was 'Tommy'), to show that, in English, we do sometimes use the French phrase 'He calls himself . . .' Have a discussion in class about which is the better phrase. Devoting attention to a point like this, highlighting the differences between these French and English phrases, helps children to understand, and remember, that the related question will be 'How do you call yourself?'

> Bonjour, bonjour,
> **Comment vas-tu?**
> Ça va bien merci,
> Ça va bien merci,
> **Et toi? Et toi?**
> Bonjour

Explain that in French we ask 'How do you go?' instead of 'How are you?', and instead of replying, 'I am well, thank you', the French phrase is 'It is going well. Thank you'.

Sometimes new words can be difficult to pronounce, so it is helpful to stress the proper pronunciation of the phrase '*Qui est-ce*'.

> **Qui est-ce?**
> **Qui est-ce?**
> C'est mon frère.
> Il s'appelle . . .
> Il s'appelle . . .
> Bonjour, bonjour.

Another song in *Le français par le chant* uses the tune of 'Happy Birthday' to introduce phrases relating to age:

First verse	Second verse	Third verse
Joyeux anniversaire,	Quel âge as-tu?	Aujourd'hui jai huit ans.
Joyeux anniversaire,	Quel âge as-tu?	Aujourd'hui jai huit ans.
Joyeux anniversaire,	Quel âge as-tu?	Aujourd'hui jai huit ans.
Joyeux anniversaire.	Quel âge as-tu?	Aujourd'hui jai huit ans.

Using songs or games to introduce different questions helps them to master the often difficult pronunciation of phrases like '*Qu'est ce que*' or '*Est-ce que*'.

Another example in *Le français par le chant* is the rap below:

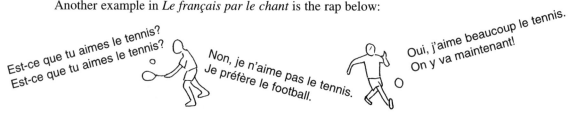

The class can make up their own rhyme by changing *le tennis* and *le football* to other sports — or even to other things they like — music, food, etc. Write a list of different sports on the board (or vary the vocabulary to practise other groups of related words). The class can use this list to invent their own versions of the rap.

Introducing rhythm breaks the monotony of the repetitive exercises essential to teaching classes how to ask questions and adds an element of fun and interest to the lesson.

Songs are often used in French teaching methods to introduce question tags and simple sentences. Below are some examples from *French start* by Teresa Scibor and *Un kilo de chansons* by Mary Glasgow Publications which are based on similar principles to the previous examples. The first is from *French start*:

> Aujourd'hui c'est lundi.
> C'est lundi, c'est lundi,
> Qu'est-ce qu'on va faire?
> Aujourd'hui, on va chez Caroline.
> Aujourd'hui, on va chez Caroline.

CiLT

Ask the class to write their own version of the song. They must choose a day of the week and can vary who they visit by changing 'Caroline' in the song, to the name of their best friend.

QUELLE EST LA DATE DE TON ANNIVERSAIRE?

Another example, this time in *Un kilo de chansons,* practises the months of the year:

Quelle est la date de ton anniversaire?	Janvier, février, mars,
Quelle est la date de ton anniversaire?	Janvier, février, mars,
Quelle est la date de ton anniversaire?	Avril, mai, juin,
Quelle est la date de ton anniversaire?	Avril, mai, juin,
Quelle est la date de ton anniversaire?	Juillet, août, septembre,
Quelle est la date de ton anniversaire?	Juillet, août, septembre,
Quelle est la date de ton anniversaire?	Octobre, novembre, décembre.
Quelle est la date de ton anniversaire?	Octobre, novembre, décembre.

As they sing, children should stand up and sit down again when the month they were born in is sung. This exercise is good for encouraging active participation in class.

These two songs are a useful way of introducing or revising days and months, and in *French start again,* another song is used to practise telling the time:

> ***Quelle heure est-il?***
> *Quelle heure est-il?*
> *Il est quatre heures*

Before the lesson, prepare a selection of clock faces showing different times, on flashcards or on the board. Encourage the class to sing the time shown on each clock face. Check their pronunciation.

 ## GAMES

QUELLE HEURE EST-IL?

The benefit of questions is that they are fundamentally interactive. They demand a response and are an essential first step in generating spontaneous conversation. Games that draw specifically on these aspects of questions are likely to be especially successful. This simple chasing game practises the question '*Quelle heure est-il?*' and revises the numbers from one to eleven.

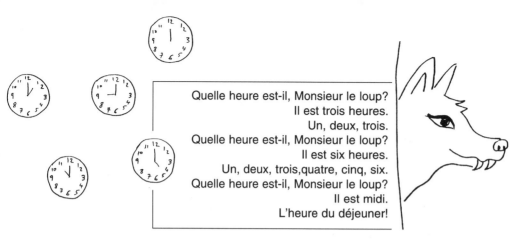

Quelle heure est-il, Monsieur le loup?
Il est trois heures.
Un, deux, trois.
Quelle heure est-il, Monsieur le loup?
Il est six heures.
Un, deux, trois,quatre, cinq, six.
Quelle heure est-il, Monsieur le loup?
Il est midi.
L'heure du déjeuner!

The children ask the question '*Quelle heure est-il, Monsieur le loup?*' to which the child who is *Monsieur le Loup* replies, either with a number — '*Il est six heures*', which the rest should then count to — or by saying that it is breakfast, lunch, or dinner-time. If *Monsieur le loup* is ready to eat, everyone should run away before he or she catches them. Whoever is caught becomes *Monsieur le loup* in turn.

'PROMENONS-NOUS DANS LES BOIS'

This is another popular French game, and is a variation on the previous game — again it involves a wolf, and is best played outside if possible. One child is chosen to be *Monsieur le loup* as before. Although the rhyme is fairly complicated, repeating it many times helps children to become familiar with some more difficult sentences, and with tense construction as introduced later in the course. Here, the most important lines are the questions at the end, and the vocabulary for items of clothing which is also revised in this example:

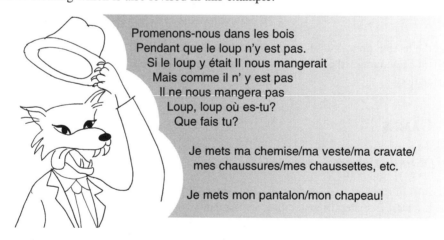

Promenons-nous dans les bois
Pendant que le loup n'y est pas.
Si le loup y était Il nous mangerait
Mais comme il n' y est pas
Il ne nous mangera pas
Loup, loup où es-tu?
Que fais tu?

Je mets ma chemise/ma veste/ma cravate/
mes chaussures/mes chaussettes, etc.

Je mets mon pantalon/mon chapeau!

Everyone sings the rhyme, and when they get to the questions '*Loup, loup où es-tu? Que fais tu?*', the wolf adds an item of clothing. The rhyme is repeated and the wolf adds another item of clothing, and so on, until he or she eventually says, '*Je mets mon chapeau*'. When they hear this, everyone else must run away, and whoever is caught becomes *Monsieur le loup* in turn.

LE JEU DES COULEURS

Questions should be used as an integral part of the course at every stage. This game illustrates how a different grammar point — one relating to colours in French — can be adapted to the formulation of questions. It can be played from very early on in the course, as the class should already be familiar with words for colour, and in this instance the format of the game is written on the board in front of them.

Firstly, write up a list of eight colours:

Before the game begins, write the following simple conversation on the board:

bleu	rouge	vert	blanc
noir	jaune	mauve	gris

Toc! Toc!
Qui est-là?
C'est moi . . .
Qu'est-ce que tu veux?
Une couleur
Quelle couleur?
Ex: Bleu..
Bravo! Tu gagnes/
Non. Recommence.

Send one child out of the classroom while the rest choose a colour. To come back into the classroom, the volunteer must knock on the door:

The class chants '*Qui est-là?*' '*C'est moi . . .*' and he or she says his or her name. The whole class chants '*Qu'est-ce que tu veux?*' and the child replies, '*Une couleur*'. '*Quelle couleur?*' asks the class. The child replies by choosing a colour, for example, '*vert*'. '*Non, c'était bleu!*' the class might reply.

The same game can be easily adapted to guess objects — the example used here is fruit. Write a list of fruit on the board beforehand. Remind the children that all fruit and vegetables ending with an *e* are feminine (*une* or *la*). The advantage of playing this game is that it involves

une pomme	une poire
une orange	une fraise
un kiwi	un melon
un citron	un raisin

everyone, and the class asks the questions **with you.** Even very shy children will participate and will benefit from the repetition of phrases and their correct pronunciation.

LES DOMINOS EN CHAÎNE

Cynthia Martin, in Young Pathfinder 2 *Games and fun activities,* has an excellent domino style game, *Dominos en chaîne,* which combines listening, speaking and reading. For this, prepare cards in sequence as follows: Mark the starter domino *Début*.

Hand cards out to pupils. It does not matter if everyone does not get a card! Say: '*On commence par ce domino-ci*' and show the card with the word *Début*.

Then start the sequence off with the trigger question. '*Bonjour, comment s'appelle-t-il?*' The pupil with the domino with the statement which matches the question, here perhaps, '*Il s'appelle Ben*', must listen and reply. He then has to ask the question which is on his domino, for example: '*Où habites-tu?*' and so the sequence is built up. This kind of practice can be made shorter for beginners, or extended as children learn more structures and vocabulary items. Dominoes can be handed on and the activity repeated with different players.

Here are some more examples.

SURVEYS

Once they have mastered the correct pronunciation of some basic questions, children should be encouraged to ask each other questions, similar to the ones practised above.

A useful way of developing this idea is by doing surveys in the class which involve everyone asking each other a particular question.

LES SONDAGES

Prepare the list of questions beforehand. They should be very simple. Divide the class into groups of six, and allocate a question to each child. Use the grids below, which should be drawn and photocopied beforehand, to explain that each child should ask their question and fill in the answers given by the other five members of the group. This ensures that everyone in the class has the chance to practise asking a question, and the format can also be adapted to revise any group of related words (here animals and transport).

Comment es-tu venu/e à l'école ce matin ?

	En voiture	En vélo	En moto	À pied	En métro	En car	En bus
Marc	☐	☐	☐	☐	☐	☐	☐
Julie	☐	☐	☐	☐	☐	☐	☐
David	☐	☐	☐	☐	☐	☐	☐
Julien	☐	☐	☐	☐	☐	☐	☐
Annie	☐	☐	☐	☐	☐	☐	☐

Cochez la case

Quel est ton animal préféré?

	Les chats	Les chiens	Les souris	Les oiseaux	Les chevaux	Les lapins	Les hamsters
Emily	☐	☐	☐	☐	☐	☐	☐
Simon	☐	☐	☐	☐	☐	☐	☐
Hollie	☐	☐	☐	☐	☐	☐	☐
Marie	☐	☐	☐	☐	☐	☐	☐
Isaac	☐	☐	☐	☐	☐	☐	☐

Cochez la case

UNE ENTREVUE

A variation on the theme is the staging of an 'interview à la Barry Jones' in class. This has the added benefit of introducing an element of performance into the proceedings. Write a list of adjectives on the board in colour-coded columns and pick out three or four of them to use in the following exercise:

in red	in blue
furieuse	furieux
folle	fou
soûle	soûl
pressée	pressé
gaie	gai
lente	lent
polie	poli
endormie	endormi
amoureuse	amoureux
inquiète	inquiet
triste	triste

Explain what each adjective means and ask the class why they think you wrote them up in two columns. Now explain that you are going to interview each child in turn.

Write three or four simple questions you intend to ask on the board. For example:

As-tu un frère ou une sœur? Quel âge as-tu? Quelle est ta couleur préférée? Quelle heure est-il?	Avec qui habites-tu? De quelle couleur est la porte? Tu aimes les chats? Qu'est ce que c'est?	Quelle est la date de ton anniversaire? As-tu un animal à la maison? Combien de crayons y a-t-il? Où habites-tu?

Choose one of the more competent speakers to start the interview, and use only one group of questions. Explain that you intend to ask these questions in one of the moods from the board, and that instead of answering normally, the volunteer must also answer in a particular mood.

Choose two different moods from the list on the board, and say, for example, that you will be 'soûl/e' and that the child will be 'fâché/e'. Write each mood on the board so that you both remember how to act.

Draw their attention to the agreement of the adjectives, depending on who is acting a particular mood. Finally, ask the questions and get the child to answer, remembering your respective moods. As the class gains confidence in answering, you can vary the questions asked, and eventually the more competent children can begin to ask the questions themselves.

This is a good way of building children's confidence in expressing themselves in French, and is lots of fun — usually even very shy children will want to participate. By adding emotions to a role play, you disguise the repetitive nature of language practice.

CILT

As with many of these exercises, it is important to prevent noisier children from monopolising the class. Make sure they know not to interrupt but to wait their turn. If anyone gets too noisy and disruptive, send them outside for a few minutes to calm down — usually children have so much fun practising these games that they will not want to stand outside for long. The exercise is a good way of filling a few minutes at the end of a lesson, and can be adapted to cover a wide range of vocabulary.

 ## GUESSING GAMES

QUI EST-CE?

Guessing games are a familiar way of practising the interrogative form — but adding a little visual material and some contemporary sparkle can make for a lot of fun.

Ask one volunteer to leave the room while the others choose one of the pictures. Give the volunteer a list of questions to ask. Using a maximum of six questions from your sheet, he or she must try to guess who was picked.

The rest of the class can only answer '*Oui*' or '*Non*' to the questions asked. Below are some examples of questions you could use:

C'est un homme?	C'est une femme?
C'est un garçon?	C'est une fille?
C'est un acteur?	C'est une actrice?
C'est un chanteur?	C'est une athlète?
C'est un athlète?	C'est une chanteuse?
Il a les cheveux . . ?	Elle a les cheveux . . ?
Il a les yeux . . ?	Elle a les yeux . . ?
Il a un grand/petit nez?	Elle un grand nez?
Il est français/anglais?	Elle est française/anglaise?
Il porte . . ?	Elle porte . . ?

DEVINE QUEL EST MON MÉTIER

Another guessing-game can be created based on the popular show 'What's my line . . ?' and is similar to other exercises from previous chapters. Divide the class into three groups, and ask one group to choose a job. The other two groups take turns to ask questions based on the grid below. Before beginning, go through any new vocabulary with them to check that everyone understands the questions they will ask. It is often helpful to read out the questions with their correct pronunciation, and to get the class to practise with you before the exercise begins:

Tu travailles à la maison?/à l'usine/à l'école/ au théâtre/ au magasin?
 au restaurant/ au stade/ à l'hôpital/ à l'église/ dans la rue?
Tu travailles le matin/ le soir?
Tu travailles seul(e)? en groupe?
Tu travailles avec les mains?
Tu es bon/ bonne en: histoire/ maths/ art/ anglais/ sciences/ sports, etc?
Tu porte un uniforme?
Tu as fait un stage? Tu es diplomé/e?

Also, write a list of professions on the board in colour-coded columns to remind the class of the vocabulary relating to different jobs (see p33).

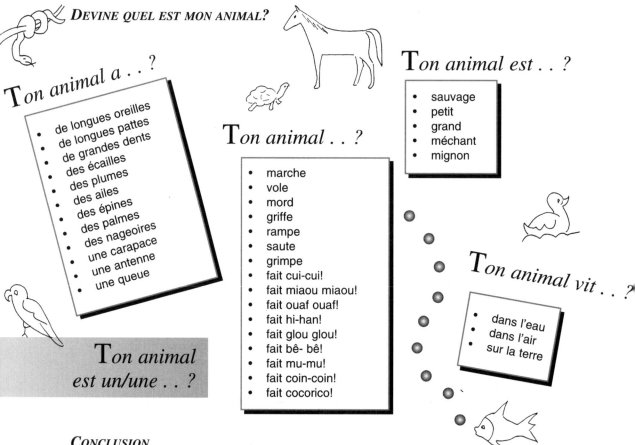

DEVINE QUEL EST MON ANIMAL?

T*on animal a . . ?*

- de longues oreilles
- de longues pattes
- de grandes dents
- des écailles
- des plumes
- des ailes
- des épines
- des palmes
- des nageoires
- une carapace
- une antenne
- une queue

T*on animal est . . ?*

- sauvage
- petit
- grand
- méchant
- mignon

T*on animal . . ?*

- marche
- vole
- mord
- griffe
- rampe
- saute
- grimpe
- fait cui-cui!
- fait miaou miaou!
- fait ouaf ouaf!
- fait hi-han!
- fait glou glou!
- fait bê- bê!
- fait mu-mu!
- fait coin-coin!
- fait cocorico!

T*on animal vit . . ?*

- dans l'eau
- dans l'air
- sur la terre

T*on animal est un/une . . ?*

CONCLUSION

Questions form the basis of much that is engaging and entertaining about learning a language: they are at the heart of dialogue. The games contained in this chapter are examples of activities that can make children forget about grammar altogether. The words they have to form become transparent; all they care about is having fun.

Conclusion

This book is an attempt to capture a philosophy of language teaching that has proved successful for many years. Its fundamental premise is that a vigorous programme of learning tasks can be delivered through the creative development of games and other engaging activities.

The book is not intended as a rigid programme that has to be adhered to, nor a series of recipes for the classroom. The games that have been described illustrate how simple and often well-known children's games can be adapted to the teaching of grammar.

No two teachers and no two groups of children are the same. What works well in one context may be less successful in another. What is important is to identify the learning tasks and select the right activities accordingly.

In the author's experience, what never fails in lessons is the transmission of enthusiasm, energy and creativity from a teacher to a classroom full of children. With a firm grasp of grammar, a willingness to communicate, and the creation of the right blend of hard work and relaxation in the classroom, a teacher can achieve almost anything. Grammar not only can be fun, it should be fun!

Bibliography

Delbende J C and V Heuzé, *Le français en chantant* (Didier, 1994). Cassette, teacher's book and pupil's book

Field D, M Forbes and A Forbes, *Le français par le chant* (Cameron Forbes, Neal, 1991). Cassette and pupil's book

Fawkes S, Pathfinder 25: *With a song in my scheme of work* (CILT, 1995)

Halliwell S, Pathfinder 4: *Yes, but will they behave?* (CILT, 1991)

Halliwell S, Pathfinder 17: *Grammar matters* (CILT, 1993)

Holmes B, Pathfinder 6: *Communication re-activated: teaching pupils with learning difficulties* (CILT, 1991)

Jeux faciles en français (European Language Institute, 1994)

Jones B, Pathfinder 10: *Being creative* (CILT, 1992)

Kay J, *Un kilo de chansons* (Mary Glasgow, 1978). Cassette, lyrics and teacher's notes

Llorca R, *Les rythmimots* (C.L.A. Besançon). CD and book

Martin C, Young Pathfinder 2: *Games and fun activities* (CILT, 1995)

Satchwell P, Young Pathfinder 4: *Keep talking: teaching in the target language* (CILT, 1997)

Satchwell P and J de Silva, Young Pathfinder 1: *Catching them young* (CILT, 1995)

Scibor T, *Zozo French party* (CYP Ltd, 1993). Cassette

Scibor T, *French start* (CYP Ltd). Cassette and pupil's book

Skarbek C, Young Pathfinder 5: *First steps to reading and writing* (CILT, 1998)

Tierney D and P Dobson, Young Pathfinder 3: *Are you sitting comfortably?* (CILT, 1995)

Tierney D and F Humphreys, Pathfinder 15: *Improve your image* (CILT, 1992)

CiLT